Wildest
AFRICA

Wildest AFRICA

Paul Tingay

NH
NEW
HOLLAND

Acknowledgements

The author would like to express his thanks to all those Africans, whether they be Mount Kenya forester, Karoo bakkie driver, Namibian Fish River Canyon official, Addis Ababa cook or Zimbabwe mountain honey gatherer, who always have the generosity, time and, above all, laughter to make the visitor feel at home. And specifically Mike and Pip Curling, Ann Tingay, Peter Joyce, Chris and Shelagh Milton, and Professor Julie Hasler.

First published in 1995 by
New Holland (Publishers) Ltd
London • Cape Town • Sydney • Singapore

4 6 8 10 9 7 5 3

24 Nutford Place	80 McKenzie Street	3/2 Aquatic Drive
London W1H 6DQ	Cape Town 8001	Frenchs Forest, NSW 2086
United Kingdom	South Africa	Australia

Copyright © 1995 in text: Paul Tingay
Copyright © 1995 in photographs: Photographers and/or their agents listed on page 6
Copyright © 1995 in maps and illustrations: Loretta Giani
Copyright © 1995 New Holland Publishers (Pty) Ltd

ISBN 1 85368 591 7

PUBLISHING DIRECTOR: Neville Poulter
EDITOR: Donald Reid
ASSISTANT EDITOR: Tracey Hawthorne
CONSULTANT: David Bristow
CARTOGRAPHY and ILLUSTRATIONS: Loretta Giani

Reproduction by cmyk pre-press, Cape Town
Printed and bound by Tien Wah Press (Pte) Limited, Singapore

Contents

Further reading

Ardrey, Robert. *African Genesis* (Collins Fontana, London)

Bonner, Raymond. *At the Hand of Man: peril and hope for Africa's wildlife* (Random House, New York)

Branch, Bill. *Southern African Snakes and other Reptiles. A Photographic Guide.* (Struik, Cape Town)

Davidson, Basil. *The Story of Africa* (Mitchell Beazley, London)

Gordon, Rene. *Africa: A Continent Revealed* (Struik, Cape Town)

Leakey, E. and Lewin, R. *Origins* (Dutton, New York)

Matthiessen, Peter. *The Tree Where Man was Born* (Dutton, New York)

Mazrui, Ali A. *The Africans* (Little, Brown and Company, Boston)

Pakenham, Thomas. *The Scramble for Africa* (George Weidenfeld and Nicholson, London)

Shelley, Steve. *Safari Guide to the Mammals of East and Central Africa* (Macmillan, London)

Sinclair, Ian. *Field Guide to the Birds of Southern Africa* (Struik, Cape Town)

Smith, Anthony. *The Great Rift: Africa's Changing Valley* (BBC Books, London)

Smithers, Reay H.N. *Land Mammals of Southern Africa* (Southern, Johannesburg)

Stuart, Chris and Tilde. *Photographic Guide to the Mammals of Southern, Central and East Africa* (Struik, Cape Town)

Williams, J.G. and Arlott, N. *A Field Guide to the Birds of East Africa* (Collins, London)

Photographic credits

Half title: *Lions mating, Timbavati, South Africa.* Title pages: *A gemsbok cow with two calves, Sossusvlei, Namibia.* Page 4: *Samburu in ceremonial dress, Kenya.* Page 5: *Cheetah and cub, early morning, Kenya.* Pages 8-9: *Giraffe at sunset, Etosha National Park, Namibia.*

$\mathcal{A}$frica map

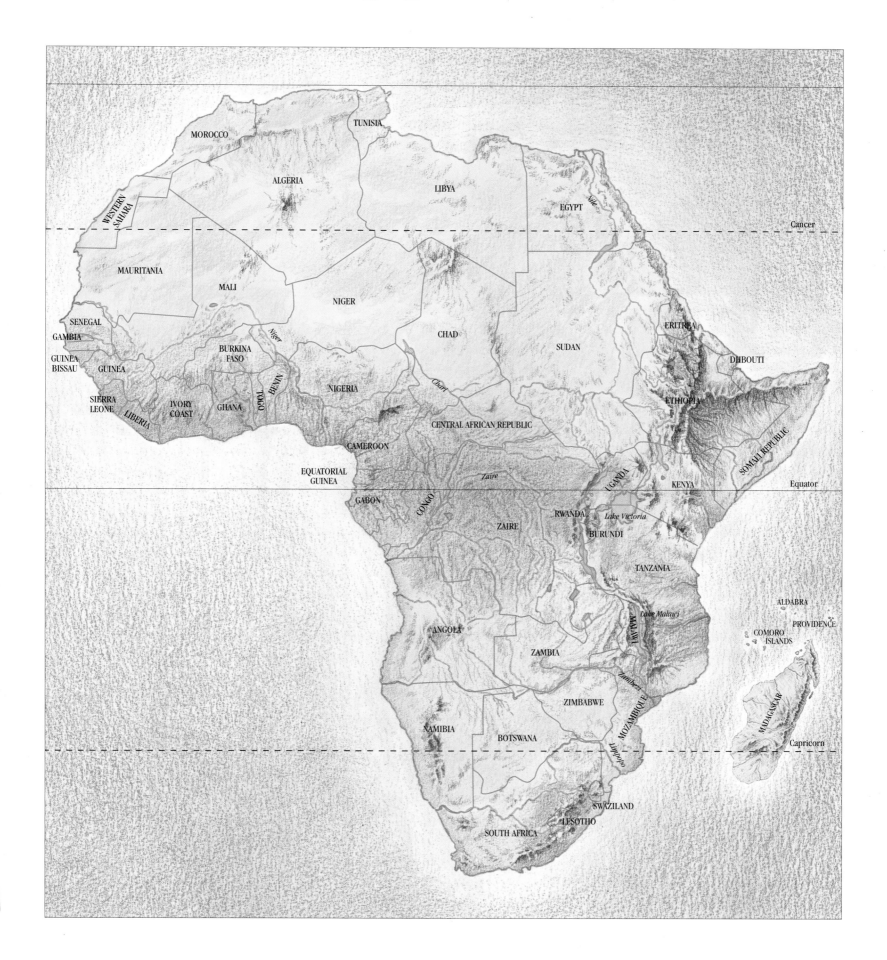

Introduction

"The ends of the earth stand in awe
The lands of sunrise and sunset."
Psalms 63, *v* 64.

L ISTEN TO THE DRUMS OF AFRICA. Hear the women's voices soft, now low the men, voices of Africa, voices from the desert, the mountains and the sea, harmonizing. They laugh, they clap, they shout for joy, they sing with the grass of the savanna as they wait for the rains. Soon, from the mountains and from the desert come the smell of dust and the first drops falling. Across the plains the zebra are thundering, and in the high fever trees the wind is calling deep on deep.

Africa, land of sunlight, space and splendour, land of elephant, lion, leopard and giraffe, stamps her imprint on your soul like nowhere else on earth. Kilimanjaro, Sahel, Karoo, Kalahari, Congo, Zambezi, Ngorongoro, Nile, Sahara, Victoria Falls, Serengeti: her very names are a powerful evocation of the wilderness and that longing that is in all of us for the wild. Perhaps on our highways, in our cities, we have forgotten our need for space and light and silence, our need for the wild. That wildness is in Africa, like the pattern of a fiery sunset, wild honey on the mountainside, or the glimpse of leopard in the mopane trees.

Africa was born, the Yoruba people of Nigeria maintain, when everything was a wasteland of marsh and moving water, where only the children of lesser gods played on spider webs strung across the void. *Ol-orun*, the Most High, arranged for solid ground to be put in its place, sent the chameleon with his big rolling eyes to observe it all, and the world was created.

Much of Africa is a high plateau sitting on a single shield of ancient rock, which in places is 3 500 million years old. At one stage it was linked to South America, India and Australia as a vast supercontinent called Gondwanaland. Now, Africa, the world's second largest continent, is linked to Asia only by a narrow strip of land. It is a landmass thirty million square kilometres in area and 8 000 kilometres long, the same length as Central and South America together.

Africa has more nations than any other continent. The Sudan, slightly smaller than India, is the continent's largest country, but jungle-thick Zaïre is almost as big, while Ethiopia, Angola, Niger, South Africa and Mali are each five times the size of the United Kingdom. The Nile in North Africa is

the world's longest river. Kilimanjaro, the snow-capped symbol of Africa's space and light is, at 5 895 metres above sea level, the world's highest free standing mountain. The Sahara, once a savanna of game, is today the world's largest desert.

Nearly everyone thinks of Africa as one entity, but the continent, large enough to swallow China, Western Europe, India and the United States, is a cosmos of many parts. Each different aspect of Africa is part of a journey through the soul of the continent. From the cool oceans off the coast of Africa's southernmost tip, the interior of Africa soon becomes a dusty, high plateau rich in mountains, wild flowers and winter snows. Crossing the muddy Orange River, you move into the vast open wilderness of the Namib Desert in the west and the Kalahari grasslands of the centre where great herds of springbok, wildebeest and zebra abound. The Zambezi River and the Victoria Falls mark the beginning of a more heavily wooded, tropical Africa; reaching the Great Rift Valley in Kenya, with its volcanoes and coconut-palm coast, you are halfway to Europe. It is on the East African plains, the Serengeti and the Masai Mara that the life-or-death struggle of migrating wildebeest and predator is continually played out. The vast drainage basin of the Congo (Zaïre) River stretches west from here – a rainforest, lush, green and almost impenetrable. North of this lies the Sahel, a long savanna belt of many cultures and nations that quickly becomes the 1 600-kilometre-wide Sahara. Finally, North Africa, with its mountains, date palms and beaches, is the warm Mediterranean land known to European travellers since the time of ancient Rome.

"The grace of creation is like a cool day between rainy seasons."
Asante praise song, Ghana.

TWO MILLION YEARS AGO, Africa was the cradle of man. Our ancestors emerged from the great forests of central Africa and stood on the open, sun-shot plains of East Africa for the first time. There were angry volcanoes flanking the Great Rift Valley, elephant larger than they had ever seen, buffalo, lion, hornbill birds and silver lakes of pink flamingos.

The first true Africans were the nomadic Stone Age hunter-gatherers who lived in many different parts of Africa thousands of years ago. Not only were they the first Africans, they were also Africa's first conservationists. Cathedrals of Stone Age art dating back thousands of years have been discovered in the great mountain ranges of the central Sahara, the Brandberg of Namibia and in thousands of aloe-strewn and boulder-tumbled overhangs throughout Zimbabwe. All reflect a symbiotic relationship between man and nature, between man and the array of animals that existed alongside him. Thousands of years ago in the areas of the Sahara that are now desert there were golden grasslands, with giraffe and oryx, leopard and elephant, and rivers of hippo and crocodile. Today the same plains are bleak and sun-ravaged, where only

Left: *A stepped pyramid at Mestapa, near Sakara in Egypt.*

Bottom left: *Tall date palms over the desert sands of Egypt.*

Below: *The landscape of rippling waves where the Saharan sand sea advances to a far, blue horizon, at Merzouga in Morocco.*

Previous pages: *A cheetah* (Acinonyx jubatus) *peers out from cover in Etosha National Park, Namibia.*

a mystic might journey to meditate or a lone Tuareg trader would pause with his caravanserai. The bleak Tassili hills of the central Sahara, wind- and sun-blasted folds of rock, searing hot by day and bitterly cold at night, contain more than 4 000 paintings and engravings. In caves and overhangs the artists show us that the Sahara 6 000 years ago was literally a land of milk, flowing rivers, pastures and honey. Combined with archaeological finds, we know that there were settled communities here earlier than anywhere else along the Nile which made pots for cooking and carrying water, and also fished with harpoons in the many rivers in the place called Tassili-n-Ajjer, which means "plateau of rivers".

Contrary to earlier belief, the first Egyptians actually came from these green savannas of the Sahara – inner Black Africa – at a time when the desert was spreading and the inhabitants of the land needed to find a more hospitable environment. The diaspora of these black nomads took some north to the well-watered Mediterranean; many went south to the rich savannas and forests; and others journeyed west to the bountiful Nile. There, two kingdoms eventually emerged and clashed on the banks of the great river, but joined under one divine king, or pharaoh, around 3200BC. Thus began the great civilization of ancient Egypt.

At the other end of the continent, right across southern Africa, there are rock paintings similar, and engravings of equal beauty, to those in the Tassili of the Sahara. They reflect the all-embracing spirituality of the San, or Bushmen as they are known, and the deep importance to them physically, symbolically and mystically of the animals of the wild.

Africans all have a tradition in their folk memory of having arrived from somewhere else. Starting three thousand years ago there was a slow but steady movement of people, farmers and craftsmen

Introduction

skilled in iron, away from the west African rainforests of eastern Nigeria and Cameroon. There were two streams: one went east, reaching East Africa by AD100 and South Africa 200 years later; the other headed south via Zambia and Angola. These migrations were not an exodus with massed columns of people on the move, but rather a long process that took about 1 500 years and, by 1800, when Europeans began exploring the interior of what to them had always been the dark and unknown continent, they found settled communities everywhere they went. Even then, Africa had a population of around 100 million people.

The civilizations of Egypt, Kush, Nubia and Axum in North Africa, Great Zimbabwe in the south, and the great medieval gold- and bronze-smelting cultures of Songhay, old Ghana, Ife, and Benin in West Africa, were all indigenous, but there have been many non-African influences down the centuries. The Phoenicians created Carthage (modern Tunis) while ancient Rome destroyed the power of Egypt, turning North Africa into the grain basket of the Empire. In the process they also devastated North Africa's game in their passion for gory gladiatorial contests between man and animals imported from Africa.

In the creation of cultures and kingdoms, both Christianity and Islam have been powerful influences in Africa. Soon after the death of the prophet Mohammed,

14

founder of Islam in AD632, Arab followers of the new religion conquered first Egypt then, within 80 years, much of North Africa and substantial enclaves along the East African coast. Meanwhile the trans-Saharan gold traders on their romantic caravans introduced Islam to the great African kingdoms of the Sahel.

There are many similarities between medieval Europe and Africa. Around the time William the Conqueror invaded England, the king of the Wolof of Senegal had an army of 10 000 horsemen; in southern Uganda subjects dared not look into the eyes of their kings; and in the south, rich cattlemen at Great Zimbabwe were building the magnificent stone structures that were to become the focal point of a city of 40 000 people. By 1450, however, a new wave of invaders, the Portuguese, were sailing down the coast of Africa intent on capturing the fabulous spice trade of the East. They were followed by the Dutch 200 years later, then the English and, in the last century, the Germans, Belgians, French and Italians.

Above: *Villagers working on the millet crop on the green, but generally low-yielding central plateau of Ethiopia.* Top left: *Looking across the mountain range of Tassili-n-Ajjer in the Sahara.* Bottom left: *An addax* (Addax naso-maculatus)*, one of the hardy species of antelope which has adapted to life in the Saharan sands.*

For Africa, its people and its game, it was to be an overwhelming 500 years. Nowhere could the Africans keep these horse-riding, musket-firing Europeans at bay; and one after the other African nations collapsed under the onslaught. A total of ten million Africans were transported out of Africa by the slave trade, along with the treasures of the pharaohs, gold, diamonds, ivory, and every manner of living creature. "Listen to the song of Africa," as Senegalese poet Leopold Sedar Senghor begs us, "listen to the beating of the dark pulse of Africa in the mist of lost villages."

"Morning has risen, Asobe God, take away from us every pain... "
Prayer of the Mbuti (Pygmy) people, Zaïre.

SET AGAINST THE BACKGROUND of colonialism, the nations of Africa did not claim a generous inheritance as they gained independence in the years following World War II. Reliant on imported oil and foodstuffs, a terrible burden was established. This inability for Africa to feed itself goes back to the European demand for colonial products – groundnuts, cotton, coffee, cocoa, tea and sugar – all of which stifled the production of foods for home consumption which the exodus from rural areas to the towns and cities exacerbated. In Africa's recent history the urban areas have called the tune at the expense of the rural heartland and have become the abyss into which money, energy, culture and peoples are disappearing.

Essentially, modern Africa is a continent in economic crisis. It does not have the mild climate or rich, fertile soil of Europe. There is sunshine and seemingly endless tropical rainforests, but Africa's soil is thin, easily baked and washed away. African farmers cannot command high enough prices from the West for their produce. They have to face the fact that 50 per cent of their continent is too dry for rain-fed agriculture, and they have an additional one million people to feed every three weeks. The continent also has a vast debt burden. For every dollar in aid, more than half goes out again in debt repayments. Per capita income is decreasing by 25 per cent in real terms every 20 years.

Africa's deficiencies are also not always relieved by outside experts. Aid donors, even the IMF and the World Bank, can do more harm than good when non-African solutions are mandated for African problems.

Yet, having shrugged off the colonial yoke and in spite of political strife, war, disease, desertification, gender inequality and a terrible urbanization process, Africa is today a continent of hope and possibility. Although largely agrarian, it does export petroleum, gold, coffee, tea, diamonds, flowers, iron ore, sugar, uranium, cotton, meat and agricultural products, tobacco, copper, fish and, from South Africa, the continent's gold-based industrial giant, manufactured goods. Tourism is expanding and becoming a significant part of the economy in many countries, a process which is slowly beginning to benefit the people of the villages, the savanna, bush and forest.

"For Zeus had yesterday to Ocean's bounds
Set forth to feast with Ethiop's faultless men
And he was followed there by all the gods."
Homer's *Iliad.*

THE ANCIENT GREEKS, founders of European civilization, considered the Ethiopians, by which they meant the black Africans as a whole, to be the "first of all men" – those believed to be the tallest and best-looking of all people. They also believed that the source of spiritual wisdom and the very names of the gods came from Africa – the epic poem of Greek culture, Homer's *Iliad*, describes how the Greek gods went each year to an Olympian banquet of the gods in the Land of Blacks.

There are some 800 different groupings of people on the continent, with many south of the Sahara closely related. Apart from the multiplicity of African languages, of which the most universal is the Arab-influenced Swahili, English, Arabic, French and Portuguese are widely spoken.

Africa's population is approaching a billion people, 75 per cent of whom live south of the Sahara, where there are also small populations of European, Indian and Arab descent. It has at least 20 cities with over a million people each; Cairo alone has a population approaching 11 million. Nigeria is the most populous country with 130 million inhabitants, equivalent to the combined populations of France, the United Kingdom and the Netherlands.

Africa has an average birth rate of three per cent, a third higher than that of any other continent and nearly twice that of the rest of the world. It has the world's lowest life expectancy, with 70 per cent of the total population living below the poverty line. Half of

the labour force is underemployed or unemployed. Only one in four Africans has access to clean water. In some countries, AIDS affects one in three adults, and there are many thousands of children orphaned by this killer disease, as well as others such as tuberculosis, hepatitis, malaria, dysentry, cholera and malnutrition. Internecine war tears nations apart, while in places such as Somalia and Ethiopia fearsome droughts devastatepopulations and turn whole peoples into refugees. Two hundred million people in Africa, possibly more, go to bed hungry each night.

But the peoples of Africa, that Africa of deserts and mountains, of rainforest and high grass savanna are, despite it all, still the most gracious and optimistic of peoples. There seems no adversity they cannot laugh at, no setback they cannot overcome, no situation that does not call for drums and clapping and music.

Above: *Wildebeest* (Connochaetes taurinus) *plunging into the Mara river during their annual migration from the Serengeti plains of Tanzania into the Masai Mara Reserve in Kenya.*
Left: *A Himba woman of the Koakoveld desert in Namibia.*

"He who does not travel will not know the value of men."
North African proverb.

NOWHERE IN THE WORLD can the beauty of so many animals in their natural habitat be seen as in Africa. In the variety and sheer exuberance of its wildlife it is the richest of all the continents. Rainforests, home of gorillas and chimpanzees, form its heartland, stretching from the Gulf of Guinea in the west to the Rift Valley, that massive fracture of lakes and volcanoes which cuts Africa in two. Savanna fans out from the forest north, east and south. Here are the great plains with wildebeest, zebra and gazelle, and the predators – lion, leopard, and hyena – that stalk them. The deserts of the Sahara and Namib lie north and south beyond the savanna, with their many life forms particularly adapted to these harsh environments.

The Sahara, however, was not always a desert. 12 000 years ago, when the retreat of the Ice Age encouraged a wetter climate, the Sahara was a green savanna of acacia trees, tall grasses, buffalo, giraffe, and lakes filled with hippo and fish. Today the Sahara is dominated in its northern regions by large dunes, and elsewhere by endless smaller rolling dune fields, or ergs, interspersed with stony plateaux called regs.

The temperature has been recorded in the Sahara at 58°C, and the annual rainfall is less than 254 millimetres. The desert stretches from the purple sands of Egypt to the Atlantic coast, a distance

of 5 150 kilometres, and south 2 250 kilometres from Tunisia to Nigeria. The Egyptian Qattara Depression is 132 metres below sea level, and in the great central Sahara mountain ranges of Tibesti, Ahaggar and Tassili, the highest peak is 3 415 metres.

In the eastern horn of Africa, Somalia's plateau slopes up to the rugged highlands of Ethiopia, a hard wilderness of sand and waddies surrounded by the warm, crystal waters of the Indian Ocean. Ethiopia, land of honey wine, ancient monasteries and silver jewellery, boasts great mountains, lakes and lush, forested valleys, which are a continuation of the Great Rift Valley. It is also the birthplace of the Blue Nile and the very latest discoveries about the origins of man.

Above: *A great silverback gorilla* (Gorilla gorilla berengei)*, among the thick vegetation of Virunga National Park in Zaire.*

Right: *Silouetted against a warm sunset, camelthorn trees stand proud in the Namib desert of Namibia.*

The people of adjacent Sudan refer to their own huge homeland as a continent rather than a country, so large and diversified is this land along the Upper Nile with its serene felucca sailing boats, red mountains at Kassala and gnarled thorn trees, with the lovely, long-legged dammah gazelle a native of the Sudan savanna.

The Sahel, the Arabic word for the southern shore of the Sahara, stretches right across West Africa to the north of the equatorial rainforest. It is a troubled savanna of green grass and heavily encroaching sands. It only has 100-600 millimetres of rain annually, which quickly evaporates. Even Lake Chad is shrivelling to a width of only 50 kilometres as the Sahara advances on a broad front, although the fringes of the lake reach out across a potential flood plain over 1 000 kilometres wide, an area surrounded by a necklace of national parks in the Central African Republic and Cameroon, the latter a country of extraordinary tropical beauty, mountains and lakes.

Around the big table mountains of Mali, only green gullies now give colour to the dusty plains but, dry as it is, sudden storms will flood rivers. Near the old medieval university town of Tombouctou, the Niger, the third longest river in Africa, 4 184 kilometres long, delineates a long loop through the wilderness of the Sahel. Rising in Guinea to the west, it twists and turns in a great northward curve which takes it through Mali, Niger and Nigeria, before spilling out into the Atlantic at the Gulf of Guinea in a huge, multi-streamed delta covering 36 000 square kilometres. Near Tombouctou the valley of the river is 500 kilometres wide.

This whole area of West Africa, although battling with the desert in the north, is a huge, green, tropical jungle along the coast from Cameroon to the palms and grasslands of Sierra Leone. It is also the most populated region in Africa and one in which the wildlife is under severe threat. The area, so often considered dark and untamed, has ironically been the centre of more civilizations and trade than any other part of Africa. To the north the Sahara dominates North Africa with an obsessive and potentially lethal embrace. The rocks, dune fields and endless pebble plains can be as romantic as Beau Geste and as searing as the harmattan winds that blow out of the wastelands. The dunes at Djebel Tadrart in Morocco, for example, are low, small and endless. Plains can sometimes be 600 kilometres long, with only the occasional crunch of collapsed boulders or strange mushroom outcrops, such as those south of Agades in Niger, to break the monotony, or sometimes mountains or djebels, burnt black by the wind and terrible heat, but which take on a silhouetted gentleness as the sun dies away in fiery glow.

A variety of animals have adapted to the desert conditions. The white-and-brown-coated, heavily built addax, with its dark eye patches, can live even in the erg seas of sand dunes and never need to drink, getting all its liquid requirements from the scant vegetation it eats. The discovery of oil has, however, breached the big antelope's last retreat deep in the desert and he may soon be extinct. Long-eared desert hedgehogs, solitary locust hoppers, big-jawed antlions, mouse-like jerboas, skinks and side-winding snakes are some of the other incredible creatures that have adapted to a life without water in the Sahara.

CREATURES THAT NEVER WORRY about an oasis, fuel or stars to navigate by are migratory birds. Twice a year, up to 180 species of birds from Europe and Asia cross the Sahara to winter in the warm south — wheatears, for example, heading for Ethiopia, or yellow wagtails to the insect-rich acacia scrub of Lake Chad and beyond. It has been estimated that five billion birds migrate to Africa each year, some going down the Nile, but the majority taking the 1 600-kilometre trans-Sahara route. To do this the birds put on deposits of subcutaneous fat to serve as fuel energy, some doubling their weight in three weeks. Barred warblers with their yellow staring eyes choose to make for the Red Sea and Lake Turkana in Kenya, while storks, eagles and bee-eaters seem to love the thermal air currents that waft around the giant volcanic plugs of the jagged mountains that protrude from the undulating hills of the Rhumsiki Plateau in Cameroon, and chestnutbanded plovers, sandpipers and terns make the long journey south to the warm waters of Walvis Bay in distant Namibia.

The very north of Africa has been ruled by Roman, Arab and, in recent times, French, German and Briton. Although flanked by the great empty quarter of desert and the daunting Atlas mountains, this ancient region called Barbary is a green, and reasonably well-watered strip of warm beaches, date palms, vineyards and fields of red wild poppies. Here in ancient Carthage, where Saint Augustine studied, there are ancient colosseums, Roman aqueducts (one 50 kilometres long), and sedate pink flamingos wading in and filtering the shallow waters.

"...Lord, let me reach next year."
Song of the Dogon people, Mali.

A T THE OTHER END of the continent, where the southern Atlantic meets the Indian Ocean, the very south coast of the continent is a series of pristine, tide-washed beaches, with roll after roll of waves disappearing in the sea mist past forested dune and lagoon to far off mountains, blue and cloud-fringed in the morning haze. It is a wilderness of gentle river lagoons, giant green cliffs where the tides surge, endless empty beaches, whales, tidal pools and wheeling sea birds. It is also a wilderness that can be cold, harsh and deadly – as it is along the empty fog-shrouded beaches of Namibia's Skeleton Coast where the Atlantic never ceases its attack, or in the wilderness of huge, forested shore dunes on the Natal coast where the only movement is that of the breaking waves and dolphins playing out at sea.

Veld or, more correctly thorn tree bushveld, is the local word for the savanna that covers much of the hinterland of South Africa. In places such as the Karoo, the veld is a flat, stony wilderness of wind-dusted bushes, wild flowers, looming flat-topped mountains and hushed silence at night. Its heat and open spaces, almost desert-like, are daunting at first but those who come to know its moods and mystery consider it to be one of the loveliest refuges in Africa. Less than a hundred years ago the largest herds of game ever known to man used to migrate across the Karoo, 10 million springbok in columns 25 kilometres wide and 150 kilometres long. The veld also describes the sands of the Kalahari where bat-eared foxes listen at giant termite mounds, and the thickly wooded hot lowveld of the Kruger National Park, not far from the snow-capped Drakensberg mountains, brims with game and is one of the best-preserved wilderness sanctuaries in Africa.

Eastern Africa's coastline is tropical, its beaches lined with fidgeting palms and coral reefs. But much of the interior of Africa is dry, giving the sky a bleached brilliance so characteristic of the continent. Gradually, as you move to the west in the southern portion of the continent, acacia and mopane woodland becomes grass, thorn trees, savanna, Kalahari sand and, finally, the desert of the Namib, the place of a thousand mountains, valleys and ochre sands where the light beckons across the dunes, pink, green and pastel brown. On the wind waves of the knife-edged crest, a desert-adapted barking gecko cackles and echoes its call before diving into the sand. At dawn, chariots of flame race across the mountain tops touching and lighting the jagged lava mountains of the Naukluft, praising and harmonizing the great spaces absolved by the sun. A crimson dune, lit one side by the sun and shadowed the other, stands impeccable. You catch your breath as a gemsbok, dark and light, stands preening its rapier horns on the crest, brazen, proud and beautiful.

To the north of the Namib, the world's oldest desert, beyond the tumbled boulders that nineteenth-century English poet Rudyard Kipling called the granite of the ancient north, lie the nations of Botswana, Zambia and Zimbabwe – the great spaces washed by the sun. Crossing the spaces, there are a hundred tree-lined rivers: Kavango, Kuando, Linyanti, Chobe, Luangwa, Shire and, above all,

Above: *The deep colour and sharp lines of one of the massive dunes at Sossusvlei, Namibia.*
Top right: *Looking across Devil's Cataract to the Main Falls at Victoria Falls, Zimbabwe.*
Bottom right: *An African fish eagle* (Haliaeetus vocifer)*, watchful over a fish at the Okavango Delta in Botswana.*

the mighty Zambezi and the *Mosi oa Tunya*, the smoke that thunders, or the Victoria Falls, a cataclysmic mile-wide avalanche of thundering water and billowing spray, rainbowed in filigree silver and fringed with delicate mist forest. Of these rivers of the wetland areas, only the Kavango does not flow into the Zambezi. The Okavango Delta, with their ilala palms, lilies and myriad crystal waterways, are where the waters of the river choke and die in the deep, deep sands of the old Kalahari. Then, on delta and desert, night falls. African night, horizon-to-horizon night, silhouetted foothills to crimson lace trees, blood orange and blue and gunmetal iron. A cold night, the sky an eternity, fired by a million ice crystals of distant light.

The Great Rift Valley stretches the length of East Africa, through Ethiopia, Kenya, Tanzania and as far south as Mozambique. Millions of years ago Africa tried to split itself asunder, buckling, rending and, when the terrible upheavals settled, leaving a great crack of volcanoes, deep lakes, snow-capped mountains and huge grass savannas teeming with all the wild animals of Africa: wildebeest, zebra, Thompson gazelles, lion, hyena and wild dog. Kilimanjaro slumbers in snowy sleep as fever trees sparkle in the fiery dawn and a pair of bateleur eagles all royal red and black and white, dive and plunge like aerial tumblers. Light touches the crater rim, a necklace of cloud below, as giraffe, black-mottled and gold, nibble on high acacia trees and elephant move royally across the great plain, the air sweet and pungent with flower.

Great ranges of volcanic, snow-tipped mountains, the Mitumba, Virungas and Ruwenzoris, divide Lake Victoria and the highlands of East Africa from the swollen Congo River and the lush green

rainforest of Zaïre that stretches to the Atlantic and around the bulge of West Africa. In the Ruwenzoris, also known as the Mountains of the Moon, gorillas like to feast on shoots of bamboo. Barrel-chested, silver-backed and with their serious brows, they catch your eye, watching, wondering, smiling. Here on the high slopes the Nile is born, there are ferns and flowers and great trees, many tressed lobelia and often the hum of bees. The peaks seem to float in the sky like fairy-tale castles, flush with ice and mist above the lakes and rainbows and bearded trees. The thick rainforests below are also home to shy, amber-coloured bongo, striped okapi, chimpanzees, elephant, leopard, tree orchids, goliath frogs, fruit-eating bats, spotted genets with their long black and white tails, and a thousand gorgeously coloured peafowls, blue fairy flycatchers and green

crested touracos. The jungle canopy above can be 20 metres thick, which allows only five per cent of the sunlight to trickle through to the forest floor where there are mosses, lichens and a million living things. Great rivers and tributaries twist and loop past waterfalls and high jungle walls, where the only form of transport is the dugout canoe and where man, who needs to plant his crops and eke out a meagre living, lives in constant competition with the diminishing jungle.

"The eternal captures men and women from fertile lands and demands of them that they make a desert in their hearts."
Frère Robert. Facing Mount Kenya.

THE STRUGGLE BETWEEN LIFE and death has always been the pivotal one in Africa. It is not just lion bringing down a buffalo in the Mara or a fish eagle snatching a tigerfish in Lake Kariba's shallows. The savanna, the coasts, the deserts, the veld, the forest and the rivers – the very wilderness itself – is facing a life-and-death struggle, with man. Trees are being cut down, the rhinos slaughtered, the cities burst with new arrivals from the rural areas. And the wilderness, that precious entity so vital to man's emotional and spiritual survival as a species, is being inexorably ploughed under. Forests are disappearing at the rate of 3.6 million hectares a year, with 6 500 hectares of savanna being cleared daily, and the Sahara is advancing at a frightening pace. The demand for firewood, the vital staple of rural people, will double in Africa in the next 20 years. Man is the most adaptable of all species, the

Below: *A large herd of elephant* (Loxodonta africana) *in Botswana, one of the few African nations where it is seen in such numbers.*
Right: *In the arid grasslands of the Kalahari in southern Botswana, wild dogs* (Lycaon pictus)*, among the continents most endangered carnivores, feed at a kill.*
Following pages: *A pair of male lions* (Panthera leo) *drink thirstily from a waterhole in the Kalahari, South Africa.*

most nomadic, the most capable, and he will undoubtedly wipe out every last source of nourishment, animal and tree, in order to survive. Ironically, therefore, man demands to be given priority, because by the time he dies of starvation the animals of the wild will have long gone.

"There is an interdependence between man and his environment," twelve-year-old schoolgirl Victim Mangena wrote, "if one cares for his and the other care not, a spark of war is born." Nothing works if we care nothing for each other. Elephant, wild dog, whale, savanna and river cannot be saved in isolation. Somehow, in a world of war and want, riches and poverty, we have to find the means to learn to care for each other, because only if man receives caring from his own species does he begin to care for his environment and for the wild.

One answer to threats is the technique conservationists have come to call "campfire". Tourism currently employs more than ten per cent of workers worldwide, and is the world's fastest-growing industry. Tourism is vital to Africa's wildlife, as are the small farmers, the fabric of Africa who live near or in the wildlife areas, and who have a stake in its survival. In Swahili, the word "safari" means "to walk", or "to go on a journey". But if the small landowner, the pastoralist or the herdsmen, whose own natural habitat is the wild and whose nearest neighbours are the creatures of the wild, is to save the trees from being firewood, dismantle his game traps, influence the city elites and keep destructive development at bay, then he must have a stake in safari.

Thus the natural reconciliation between our love for the wilderness and the small farmer's hope for an economic stake could result in a shared campfire of survival whereby rural communities in Africa manage their own wildlife, reap the financial benefit and preserve the game for us all. And in all of this Africa, this wilderness harmony of silence and sunlight, loneliness need not be a city of millions and compassion can be a new face. Conservationists will have to decide if hunting as a factor in ecotourism is a good or bad thing, tourism operators may need to look more closely at the fragile environment to which they bring their visitors, and African politicians may need to remember their ancestors and the ancestral savannas of their youth.

And those who live in more fertile, fortunate lands, but who yearn for the great spaces, could do much to help, even if it is only to know a continent that, although wounded by man, retains a special healing power of its own. The ability to take us back to something perhaps long forgotten, to the simpler, gentler rhythms of existence and "to a stillness," as the Mutemwa poet John Bradburne worte, "where our souls find their true eloquence". And if we hear the drums, this soon becomes a praise song not only to Africa, to its beauty and its tranquillity, but also to our own participation in this exuberant, wildest, Africa.

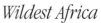

Rift

WHEN THE RAINS OF AFRICA *were still young, millions of years before man walked on the land, the huge African continent tried to tear itself asunder in a volcanic frenzy that left a jagged valley 7 000 kilometres long from the Dead Sea in Israel to Lake Malawi, far into southern Africa. Created in the awful upheaval were volcanoes, rivers, hot springs, lakes and vast plains that still support fully half of all Africa's big game. On the edge of this great rift, a child of the turbulence and mantled in permanent snow, Kilimanjaro looks down onto the endless grasslands of game on the border that divides Kenya and Tanzania. The Rift Valley has long been the majestic heartland of all that Africa means to many, yet always it has something new, always that capacity to surprise and, in its wild, majestic beauty, always that power to inspire.*

Patterns of survival

"O GRANT ME A GIRDLE O GOD," the praise-song of the Samburu goes, "multi-coloured with sons and daughters..." On the lava plains of the Rift Valley facing Mount Kenya, young Samburu herdsmen, above right, decorate and adorn themselves with the same natural instinct for camouflage as the cheetah and giraffe, whose endless vistas they share in a harmony of light and space, death and life. The word "samburu" means "butterfly", a deft compliment to these proud, ochre-painted pastoralists of the plains.

Also patterned for life in the bush is the reticulated giraffe (*Giraffa camelopardalis reticulata*), above, so called for its patchwork colouring and the old Arabic name *xirapha*, "one who walks swiftly". Arabs in search of ivory and gold were trading across the Sahara and in East Africa 1 500 years ago, not long after the Romans were abducting animals such as the cheetah for their gladiatorial spectacles in the Colosseum.

In open country the cheetah (*Acinonyx jubatus*), right, will walk virtually right up to its prey, pausing motionless now and again to allay the suspicions of its nervous target. When panic-gripped prey does take flight, the cat hurtles into action. Shoulder muscles bunched like pistons, tail rigid to counter the twists and turns of the chase, it can reach 100 kilometres an hour with bounding strides seven metres long.

PREVIOUS PAGES: *Africa's sun dies to dusty sleep across the endless plains of the Serengeti in Tanzania.*

$\mathscr{S}$ilent shores, silent world

T HE LIGHT AND SPACE OF AFRICA are never more eloquently crystallized than on its tropical shores. Three hundred kilometres east of the Rift, the East African coast, right, is a place of lagoons, fidgeting reef breezes, bougainvillea and spindly coconut palms burnt by salt and sun, swaying in the trade winds. A sleepy coast of powdery sands and fishing dhows, perfumed islands and historic conquest, the land of *zanj*, or blacks, as it was called for centuries, was the birthplace of the Swahili culture and language which are now dominant throughout East Africa.

Beyond the reefs, a rainbow world of silence seems to hold evolution hostage in a constant panorama of colour, strange shapes and hypnotic movement. The coral reefs that fringe Africa's shores, from the Red Sea south as far as the Zululand coast of South Africa, form oceanic gardens of angelfish, spiny urchins, brilliantly spotted cowrie shells, stag corals, moray eels, parrot fish and fierce barracudas.

The oriental sweetlips (*Plectorhinchus orientalis*), below, is sometimes called a grunt from the noise it makes when grinding its teeth. It changes colour dramatically as it matures into an adult, its horizontal stripes giving way to spots. When attacked by predators, a scenario as familiar in underwater Africa as it is on land, sweetlips swarm, school, and take amazingly agile evasive action.

ℒife and death on the Serengeti

TWICE A YEAR IN THE SERENGETI, an area of golden grass plains flecked with blue hibiscus flowers in the rainy season, two million animals – zebra, Thompson's gazelle and, most strikingly, wildebeest – set off on a trek up the strip of land between the Rift Valley and Lake Victoria in northwestern Tanzania in search of grazing. What is essentially a simple quest for food becomes, with Africa's enduring knack for drama, one of the great spectacles of the wild. The wildebeest columns are sometimes forty kilometres long and their migratory instinct so powerful that they will hurl themselves off a bank into a swollen river rather than detour to avoid danger. Consequently many are drowned, left, providing fast food for watchful crocodiles, lion and other predators who hungrily monitor the great crossing.

Although they are one of the predators of the animals in the passing herds, leopard (*Panthera pardus*), with an impala kill, above, are seldom seen. They are stealthy killers, often hunting by night and sometimes using tree lairs from which to pounce on their prey. The kill, occasionally weighing as much as the leopard itself, is invariably dragged away and secreted up a chosen tree.

*H*igh skies of the Mara

IN EAST AFRICA, WITH ITS ENDLESS thirsty plains and high skies, the dust hovers and filters the light, and on days when the massed thunder clouds gather, the horizon from end to end turns gun-metal grey and burnished gold in sunsets of breathtaking splendour. But on the equator the sun is quickly gone and there is little time for a lone zebra, right, to rejoin its herd before predators begin to prowl the night.

For the solitary Maasai herdsman below, however, endlessly searching for grazing for his plodding zebu cattle on plains crazed by drought, the coming of evening, or even a thorny acacia, would be welcome respite. To the nomadic Maasai people, who dominate the areas around the Serengeti and its extension in southwestern Kenya, the Masai Mara Game Reserve, cattle are God-given and central to a person's prestige and importance. Tall, striking and recognizable by their wrapped red blankets, the Maasai hold on to this traditional way of life with a proud tenacity born of their long relationship with and deep understanding of the land.

Tormented Turkana

THE GREAT RIFT VALLEY is clearly visible from the moon, a long jagged scar down the right side of Africa. As the earth cracked and opened down this fault millions of years ago in the convulsions of a continent on the move, great lakes were formed. One was Lake Turkana, left.

Its jade green waters shimmer in searing 54°C heat, reflecting the arid desert, lava plains and volcanoes of Kenya's northern border with Ethiopia and Sudan. The narrow, 250-kilometre-long lake cuts through a wilderness of scrubby bush and stinging sands where gales, as if born in the fires of hell, howl in from the wastelands to torment the waters and doum palms of the lakeside. Smoke rises ominously from Central Island's craters, where the lakes and wild fruit trees attract hordes of birds migrating south from Europe, while on South Island parts of the craters glow periodically at night, lit by the volcanic embers deep down beneath the ash that shrouds the island. Lake Turkana has the world's largest concentration of crocodiles, which are still fearlessly hunted by members of the El Molo tribe, such as the boy below fishing on the shores at Loyangalani. Although the land is harsh and inhospitable, fossils discovered near the lake by Kenyan scientist Richard Leakey, building on the work done by his parents farther south in the Rift Valley at Olduvai Gorge, confirm that man was living in the area well over a million years ago.

$\mathcal{N}$omads of the Rift

G USTS OF GOLDEN STEAM envelop long-legged flamingos (*Phoenicopterus minor*), right, feeding at dawn on the thermal hot-spring lake of Bogoria, another of the chain of sun-blasted lakes in the Rift Valley. The soda-rich waters of the lake, born of volcanic ash, breed algae, ready food for a population of over four million flamingos, 70 per cent of the world's total.

Flamingos, with their two-metre-long knobbly legs, pink plumage, tomahawk beaks and sinuous necks that they twist into figure-of-eight contortions, can be seen in their hundreds of thousands foraging for food at the lake's edge or flying past in massed formation. Lake Natron, a little farther south in Tanzania, is the world's largest breeding ground, but in fact these beautiful birds are compulsive wanderers. In pursuit of the microscopic algae that flourish on flooded salt pans, they migrate to the vast Makgadikgadi salt pans near the Okavango Delta in Botswana, to Etosha Pan and Walvis Bay in Namibia, and to Lake St Lucia and even Cape Town in South Africa. They can also be found in India, Europe and South America.

The Maasai tribesman above would once have killed a lion to justify his headdress mane, or *olawaru*, although now such practice is rare. At the *eunoto* ceremony marking his transition from the ranks of warrior to the marriageable elderhood, the ritual chalk designs on his face and body remind his male contemporaries and admiring womenfolk of his deeds of bravery.

The migration

TRIGGERED BY THEIR THEIR PARTIALITY for wet spring grass, which they seem to smell from vast distances, more than a million blue wildebeest (*Connochaetes taurinus*), below right, migrate twice annually across the Serengeti plains on the western side of the Rift Valley. Following the progression of the seasonal rains which water and renew the grass plains, they travel in an 800-kilometre circuit accompanied, as often as not, by up to half a million tail-swivelling Thompson's gazelles and 200 000 zebra outriders. Blue wildebeest are actually a dusty silver grey colour. These kicking, snorting, horn-tossing, hyperactive clowns of the plains are also known as gnu, from the old South African Khoikhoi word for the startled "ge-nu" bellow the wildebeest makes when alarmed. Their migrations coincide with the mating and, later, the calving seasons, the one exceptionally noisy as the dominant bulls fight over and mate with practically all the females, the other a miracle of massed birth. Within five minutes of being born the calves can run almost as fast as their mothers. They need to: predators, including lion,

cheetah, hyena and widely distributed leopard, are never far away. Lion regularly feast on both wildebeest and zebra by jumping on their backs from behind, sometimes raking and tackling their rumps to fell them, then strangling their prey by clamping its throat or suffocating it with a face-on bite.

Kenya's Grevy's zebra (*Equus grevyi*) or *punda milia* in Swahili, bottom left, are taller and larger than the migratory Burchell's zebra which is common in much of the rest of Africa. They also have more stripes. Grevy's and Burchell's

zebras are often seen alongside each other in mixed herds, but the two species do not interbreed in the wild. Each zebra's stripes are unique, a phenomenon which applies equally to another set of black and white stripes seen on the plains, those of the vulturine guineafowl (*Acryllium vulturinum*), top left. With its bright blue chest and the prim body language of a disdainful maiden aunt, the rotund guineafowl is a gregarious creature, conspicuous in vegetation or during its short, hasty flight.

By the drinking hole

WATER MEANS LIFE OR DEATH to all the creatures of Africa. It is the need for fresh grass which drives the wildebeest columns across the plains of the Rift and water holes, right, that many animals, including buffalo and elephant, are often seen. Encroached upon by man and his need to plant crops, the elephant's territory has rapidly narrowed. In Africa south of the Zambezi, where there are still large herds of elephant, this is a major problem, for within the confines of a game reserve it means the elephant often devastates his narrow environment, pushing down and generally denuding trees. In East Africa the problem is poaching. The 60 000 elephant in Kenya's Tsavo National Park have been reduced to a fraction of that number, forcing local conservationists to demand a worldwide ban on the sale of ivory, an unwelcome decision in southern Africa where conservationists are adamant that the elephant will only survive if the local people who live alongside them see financial benefits in protecting the animals (from the sale of ivory, meat and hides, as well as ecotourism).

Long-necked gerenuk (*Litocranius walleri*), on the other hand, are creatures of the arid savanna which hardly need to drink, obtaining the liquid they need from what they eat. Known as *swala tiga*, or the giraffe-gazelle, in Swahili, this antelope of Somalia and northern Kenya, above, spends a good part of its time on its hind legs browsing on acacia bushes.

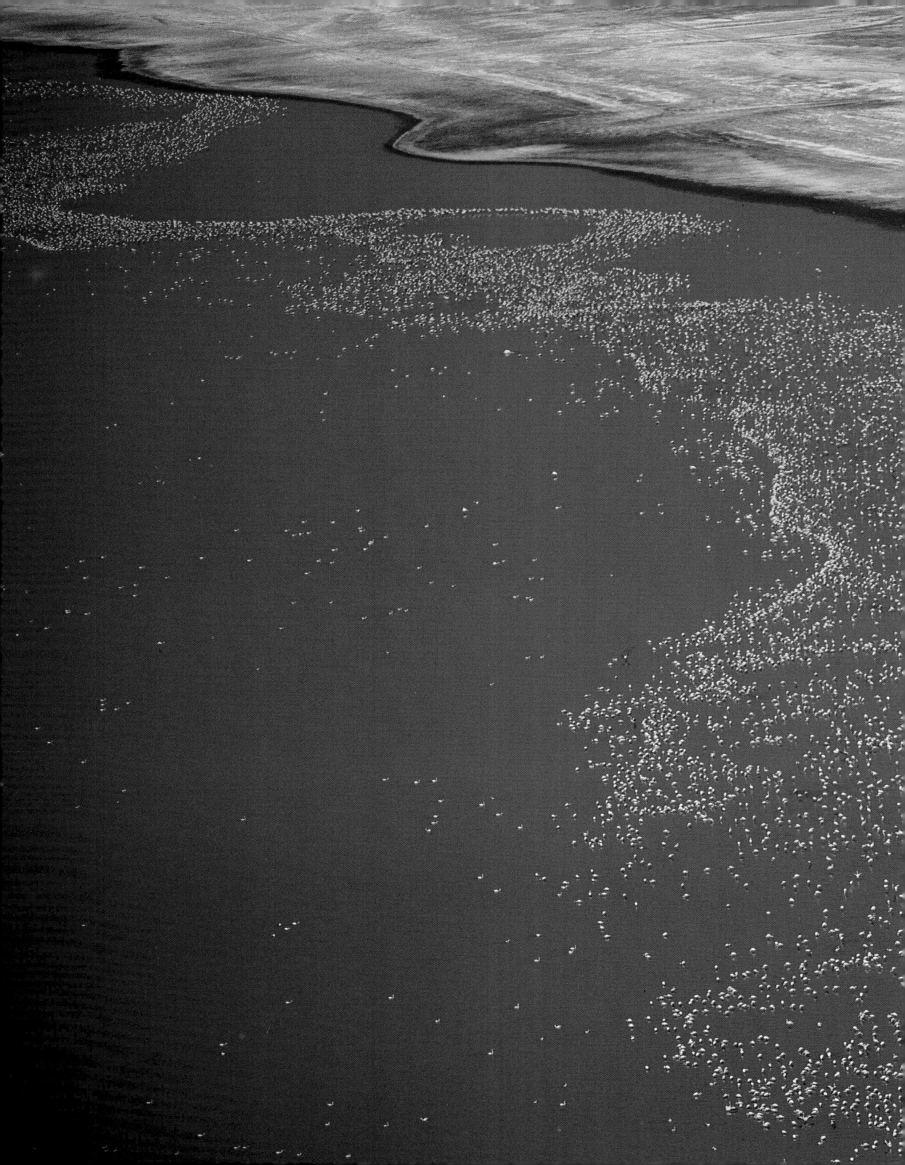

Enduring Africa

A GREAT WING OF WATER, threat or blessed relief, seems to hover behind the storm clouds which herald the long rains of the high savanna and grasslands, left. It is when the rains start, and the grass begins growing, that the great herds move northwards towards it from the Serengeti and into the Masai Mara Game Reserve in Kenya. On the horizon is the recognizable silhouette of a giraffe, an animal which browses on acacia trees and is thus less dependent on seasonal grazing variations and migratory patterns.

In such scenes there is a timelessness to the dark continent, an attitude that seems to ignore the immediacy of our modern life. On Lake Baringo, below, a boy of the Njemps tribe paddles a fishing canoe made of lightweight ambach, a pithy wood tied together with sisal. Lake Baringo is haven to an incredible 450 species of both water and acacia-bushland birds. In Kenya's Rift Valley, only Baringo and Naivasha are freshwater lakes, albeit stained these days by fine volcanic silts washed in from areas grazed by cattle and goats.

PREVIOUS PAGES: *Like a blush of pink confetti, flamingos forage in the blue waters of Lake Bogoria, a small Rift lake to the west of Mount Kenya.*

" **N** OW THIS IS THE LAW OF THE JUNGLE," wrote Rudyard Kipling, "as old and as true as the sky." The law, for all that, is a harsh one, for in the wild you grow up quickly, or die. This baby elephant, above, separated from its family, tries to escape the marauding attention of young lions learning to hunt. Normally, the highly protective female breeding herd around the elephant would make short shrift of the impertinent predators, but the youngster has wandered off too far and ultimately paid the price. The young of any species are always the first choice of and easy pickings for predators that will not only snatch them practically from their mother's womb, but also have to hide and protect their own from a similar fate. On average an adult lion will kill in the region of 19 large animals annually, working at night in well-coordinated if often unsuccessful prides. The lion (*Panthera leo*), below, was once common in Europe and Asia, as well as Africa, but the last lion was exterminated in Greece around AD100 and in Palestine about 1150. Hunt, kill, eat, survive; in Africa the law is inexorable.

Life is not always so tense, however, as this olive baboon (*Papio anubis*), right, seems to indicate as she yawns and grooms her little one in the safety of a red thorn acacia where they have spent the night. The baby baboon, with its cheeky red face, will cling tightly to its mother as she moves with the troop, ready to scatter at full speed if leopard, the main predator of adult baboons, are about.

A terrible beauty

A TERRIBLE BEAUTY AND A SERENE SAVAGERY define the wild. It is a place where yellow eyes watch in the grass, where the scent in the wind can mean life and a moment's relaxation horrible death. On this knife-edge all the animals of the wild live, at once enemies and co-conspirators. For the migrating herds, protection is found in numbers just as the fresh grasslands are sought together. The predators who follow or wait for the migration, on the other hand, will often work alone or in small numbers when hunting, although ultimately they are dependent on the herds for their prey and sustenance.

In the crush of the Serengeti migration, river crossings are fraught events. Many of the animals are taken by crocodiles and others drown, left to float down the river and, left, gladly dragged in by a pair of lionesses. Although continually preyed upon by man, lion as a species have survived reasonably well in eastern and southern Africa. Not so the glorious bush tank, the lumbering, cantankerous black rhinoceros (*Diceros bicornis*), below, a rare sight now in East Africa. International crime syndicates have methodically and mercilessly hunted down the rhino as its horn fetches astronomic prices in the Far East, where practictioners of traditional medicine believe it assists in the suppression of fevers. No country in Africa has been able to protect its rhino with the exception, to date, of South Africa. That country is the last to be targeted, but only time will tell if its politicians, conservationists, bureaucrats and businessmen can unite to resist corruption, a factor as tenacious as the poachers' weaponry, in the campaign to save the rhino.

Dark and beautiful

NOT ALL THE RIFT is an idyll of rolling plains and snow-capped mountains. In northern Kenya, Ethiopia and Somalia, large tracts of the landscape, right, are covered by sun-scorched desert and scrubland, where life is an endless search for food and water, and only the hardiest of animals and humans survive. In the bleak northlands, when a nomadic family fades from view into the shimmering desert, those left behind sing:

> "Though your way may lead through places steeped in heat, stifling
> and dry, and in a random scorching flame of wind that parches the
> painful throat and sears the flesh, may God in compassion let you
> find the great boughed tree that will protect and shade."

Lake Turkana is a bleak lunarscape of shadowed lava boulders, a hostile wilderness where crocodiles, scorpions and snakes survive as they have done, better than any other creature, for millions of years. West of the lake is the Chalbi Desert, the plains of darkness which the tough camel-herding Gabbra people of Marsabit, below, cross in search of grazing and watering points. These semi-nomadic people, speaking the Cushitic language of their Ethiopian fore-bears, emerge from the desert like the gazelle – fragile, dark and beautiful.

An army on the march

To THE TIRELESS WILDEBEEST, migration seems a stronghold in times of distress, just as it was for humans before they settled in cities. Day and night, the movement of life in the wild hardly ceases, the short African sunset catching an instant in the wind as trudging lines of dusty wildebeest, right, move across the Olympian canvas like an exhausted army returning from war. There are few other places in Africa where the animals and the landscapes they inhabit combine with such grandeur.

Observing the great movements, two bateleur scouts, above, crouch poised in a split-stemmed doum palm. The bateleur (*Terathopius ecaudatus*), with its red beak, fluffy black ruff and unmistakable black and white wings, has mythological significance in some parts of Africa, where it is considered to be the spirit messenger of the high savanna. The eagle takes its name from the French word for acrobat, the image thrown up by the bird's rocking motion in flight.

The snows of Kilimanjaro

ETERNAL SYMBOL OF AFRICA, Kilimanjaro has one fifth of all the ice in Africa in its permanent ice fields, which rise to an altitude of 5 895 metres above sea level. It is the tallest mountain in Africa and the highest freestanding summit in the world. Kilimanjaro, or "great mountain of springs", to give it one of its many names, was known by reputation to the ancient Greeks, Chinese chroniclers, Arab slavers and Portuguese transoceanic sailors, but it was not until 1848 that Western man saw snow at the equator for the first time. The first recorded conquest was in 1889.

Kilimanjaro actually consists of three extinct volcanic cones: the highest, Kibo, left, is the familiar wedding-cake pinnacle locked in ice cornices, with the lower peaks, Mawnzi and Shira, positioned on either side. The permanent ice, below, reached down to 3 000 metres above sea level in ancient times; today it starts at 5 000 metres. At this height the only signs of life are tenacious flaky lichens and the occasional weather-beaten spider.

FOLLOWING PAGES: *Mount Kilimanjaro, a serene dome rising out of thick, blanketing cloud.*

Hunter and hunted

D IFFERENT SPECIES OF ANIMAL often eat together on the plains, predators sharing a kill or grazers, such as the Grevy's zebra, below, nonchalantly walking side by side. Others literally eat off each other, like these yellowbilled oxpeckers (*Buphagus africanus*), right, searching for tasty ticks on a buffalo.

Yet the leopard, as the poet Kipling says, walks alone and all places are the same to him. Hunter of darkness, the leopard is one of the few animals to have got the measure of man. Silently, and with great cunning, it survives invisibly wherever there is food to be found, taking impala, as left, other species of antelope or the smaller grazers on the plains, rodents, fish, carrion, and even man's cattle. The tale is told of one hunter who tracked a cattle-rustling leopard for three days. What he did not know was that the leopard's mate was stalking him, a fact he realised one night when he turned on his flashlight to find both male and female charging him, one head on, the other from the rear. Leopard prefer tumbled kopjes or high trees to hide in with their kill: there they can eat alone, untroubled by scavengers, and can return regularly to the same kill.

𝒩*gorongoro*

NGORONGORO CRATER in the Tanzanian Rift is one of the world's great natural wonders. The crater floor, below, 18 kilometres across and decorated by lofty acacia trees and open vistas of grazing game, is surrounded by a pavlova rim of mountains rising 2 200 metres above sea level. The crater is surrounded by a much larger conservation area shared by both animals and Maasai pastoralists. It is a place of lake, savanna forest, swamp, recently active volcanoes, and even sand dunes, and acts as a natural throughway beside the Serengeti National Park, providing a huge area through which wildebeest, zebra and other animals migrate.

The crater was formed 2.5 million years ago when the molten lava beneath the peaked dome of a volcano cooled and subsided, leaving the roof, now with no support, to implode. What resulted was the world's largest and most exquisitely crafted caldera, an oasis of lush grazing and water that acts as a protected home for large numbers of some of Africa's most impressive inhabitants, left.

TALL ACACIA TREES in Ngorongoro crater, left, fever yellow in the light of the setting sun, dwarf the largest of beasts, the elephant (*Loxodonta africana*). The scene captures a quintessential picture of Africa: romantic, majestic, beautiful.

Life for man is often portrayed in the same terms, aloof and colourful with images of noble warriors striding across the plains. The reality, however, is often very different as Africa struggles to survive urbanization, desertification, inadequate returns on goods exported to the West, and appalling economic, medical and population strains. Despite the colourful beads of this Turkana girl, above, and the brave show of a young Samburu boy, below, the continent is weeping. For the people of the land where man began, the crops often fail, shelter is inadequate, the trees are falling and, it seems, there is only gall to drink.

Flamingo flotilla

PARTYING ON THE SHALLOW LAKE of Ngorongoro's crater floor, left, a flamingo flotilla adds a spectacular splash of soft colour to the often barren African landscape. The massive birds are flying filtration plants, sucking in water, hiving off algae nourishment, and simultaneously pumping the soda-poisoned water out again with their tongues. Such a diet includes carotenoid pigment, also found in garden carrots, which gives flamingos their blushing colour. Without it they are, so to speak, no longer in the pink, a whiter shade of pale making them less attractive to the opposite sex.

The elusive leopard, while not changing its spots, does vary its colour codes according to its exceptionally wide range of habitats. In East Africa leopards give birth after a gestation period of approximately 100 days. Normally a mother will produce a litter of two or three cubs, which are blind at birth but by the age of four months will go hunting with their mother, following her white curled tail in the long grass. When she gives a low vocal signal, they will freeze and watch as she moves in for the kill. Even when the cubs leave their mother at about two years of age, they never seem to lose the affectionate relationship of their youth and reunions are joyous affairs. There is nothing more appealing in the wild than a creature playing with its young, and even a fierce killer such as this leopard mother and cub, below, is no exception.

PREVIOUS PAGES: *Ngorongoro, the place said to be named after a Maasai cattle bell maker, seen from the crater rim. In the centre is Lake Magadi.*

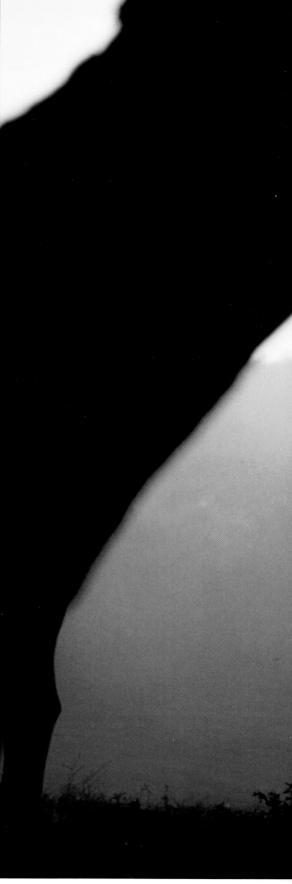

Z EBU, RIGHT, THE ANCIENT HUMPED CATTLE of East Africa, are believed to have originated in Asia as the *banting* or *gayal*. Today they are part of the constant battle to survive for the ordinary African herdsman, to whom drought and dust, searing heat and cold, are daily and bitter bread.

It is in the volcanic valleys between Ngorongoro and the Serengeti plains that the secrets of man's first struggles with the land that must sustain him are held. Underneath the ash thrown out by Kerimasi volcano on the Laetoli plains, scientist Mary Leakey in 1978 discovered the 3.7-million-year-old footprints of an upright-walking hominid family. Earlier discoveries in nearby Olduvai Gorge by her husband, Louis, confirmed that the 1.7-million-year-old *Homo habilis*, or "Handy Man", was capable of making tools, and is quite possibly a direct ancestor of modern man.

For the creatures of the wild such as the lithe and supple cheetah, above, with its amber eyes and splendid facial markings, ready to tear away at the slightest hint of danger, the parameters of territory and food are also narrowing. Man and beast, competing for shrinking land, are inextricably united in the inevitable suffering that too little room in the African ark entails. The harsh consequence of this is violence to the animals. And a kind of dying in the soul of man.

ELEPHANT PREFER TO LIVE in family groups made up of an adult female with young, or a larger group of closely related females, together with their youngsters. Such an arrangement is commonly referred to as a family breeding herd. Bulls become part of the family scene only when the females invite them in for mating. Soon they are sent off again to rejoin bachelor herds or, in the case of older bulls, to live on their own. The leading female is the matriarch of the whole herd, which can number several hundred. When young males reach puberty they leave the herd. The elephant above are in savanna with doum palms, the only member of the palm family to split and grow branches. Elephant are particularly fond of the three-cornered orange-brown fruit of the doum, the seeds of which they help to disperse in their large piles of dung.

The green tree snake (*Dispholidus typus*), top right, or boomslang in South Africa, is a day hunter. It is partial to birds, eggs, chameleons, and generally any creature foolish enough to dally on a branch where the snake lies disguised, waiting. The green tree snake's venom, a potent haemotoxin, prevents blood from clotting, but as its fangs are positioned far back in its mouth the poison is released only once the snake starts to chew its prey.

Red hartebeest (*Alcelaphus buselaphus*), right, are a plum-coloured antelope known as *kongoni* in Swahili, with a variety of subspecies in East Africa. They live in large herds in all the drier lands south of the Sahara, including Kenya, Senegal, Botswana and Namibia. Largely independent of water, they will migrate long distances in search of grazing.

Desert

ONLY THE HIMBA, *hardy nomads of Kaokoland, and fleet-footed predators such as the elegant cheetah survive in the lava-blackened mountains, mighty dunes and ancient pebble plains of the southwestern corner of Africa. Under the searing heat of the sun, the desert of sand and rock does not stir, waiting like a gecko, motionless. Above, the sky is an eternal blue, sealed by neither horizons nor heavens, and to each turn the arid landscape shows no sign of comfort or hope. A few animals, reliant only on scarce and precious water or nature's own resourceful confidence, make a home of the desert. The beauty they share is a harsh, severe beauty, a beauty sculpted from light and space and austerity. Their home is a barren wilderness, a land burnt brown by the sun, a land, they say, God made in anger.*

The dry land

THE DRY THIRSTLAND THAT STRETCHES inland from Namibia's Atlantic shore is a vast, harsh desert that was formed 80 million years ago. In some areas the sweeping winds have sculpted classic dunes and furrowed fields of red sand; in others the land seems to be huge and inhospitable, a place where you would not expect to see any form of life. Nature, however, is enormously resourceful.

In Damaraland, an arid region adjoining the bleak and hostile Skeleton Coast, a number of animals which are more commonly associated with the green African bush have, in one way and another, adapted to life in the harsh ochre sands. These include elephant, rhinoceros, bottom, and giraffe, left, the remnant populations of herds which have been forced into the desert by diminishing habitats and the constant threat of poachers.

For an animal which so revels in water, the desert is hardly an easy place for an elephant (*Loxodonta africana*), drinking below, to exist. Elephant are members of the Proboscidea order, those animals with long, flexible, prehensile trunks, which elephant use to suck up water to squirt into their mouths, or to spray over their bodies to cool down.

PREVIOUS PAGES: *A desert-dwelling elephant, wandering through the hard, forbidding and unusual landscape of the Kaokoveld in northwestern Namibia.*

$\mathscr{P}$anic at the pan

THE ARID REGION OF THE SOUTHWEST has many ironies. As the fog rolls in from the cold south Atlantic Ocean each night into the dips and hollows of the dunes, the parched Namib becomes the world's most humid desert. When the summer rains come, long sand rivers and bone-dry canyons transform into raging torrents for a few blessed hours each year. Meanwhile, in the north, natural springs surround Africa's largest, driest and saltiest pan, the Etosha.

The springs and woodland scrub of the pan attract thousands of animals. Drinking alongside giraffe and zebra, right, these curly-horned kudu (*Tragelaphus strepsiceros*) appear to have sensed a predator as they start up in panic at a water hole. Different animals all have different drinking times in Etosha. Kudu and eland like a pint or two in the morning, zebra are normally lunchtime imbibers, elephant prefer late afternoon, while giraffe will grace any gathering. Lion drink at night and hyena in the small hours after midnight.

Tall, severe-looking secretarybirds (*Sagittarius serpentarius*), below, take their name from the sprig of quills they have as head and tail feathers. They feed mainly on insects, but will also eat small mammals, snakes and other reptiles. These they lance with their bill, then stamp on to soften up before swallowing whole.

$\mathcal{L}$*ife and death, chained together*

BUTTER-YELLOW FLOWERS AND FRESH SPRING GRASS bloom alongside the sun-bleached bones of a zebra on the Beiseb plains of the Etosha Pan, left. Life and death share the same spaces in Africa, joined together in the cycles of drought and rain that grasp the soul of the plains and deserts alike. The pan, 120 kilometres long and 55 kilometres wide, is usually a blinding expanse of dust and shimmering mirages, parched and hostile. When the new-year rains come they bring both water and life, though even then the waters of the lake formed in the pan are twice as salty as seawater and only itinerant flamingos and a few hardy amphibians flourish in their algae-rich shallows.

Revelling in the lushness of the wet season, giant green and gold bullfrog (*Pyxicephalus adspersus*), above, produce a raucous cacophony in their bellowing for female attention. The female lays up to 4 000 eggs, and within three weeks the wetlands are alive with tiny, piping bullfrog.

Shades of grey

IN THE HARSHNESS OF THE SANDS and high skies of Namibia, the austerity of black and white seems particularly fitting. It is a cloak shared by creatures of the land as disparate as Burchell's zebra (*Equus burchelli*), above, and the flap-neck, or common, chameleon (*Chamaeleo dilepsis*), right. The mysterious reptile does, however, have many other colours from which to choose — its enormous range of camouflages varies from leopard spots to dark green to the metallic flintiness of the salt pans. The changes are partially dependent on the reptile's level of excitement or fear and are often used to regulate body temperature. Chameleons are lovely creatures, with eyes that swivel independently as they rock back and forth, advancing slowly along a tree branch or path. Many in Africa hold the chameleon in awe and are very reluctant to touch one for fear of bad luck. When disturbed, the male flap-neck chameleon puts on a grand show, inflating itself, hissing, opening its large, orange-lined mouth and raising its dinosaur-like neck flaps. For all the performance, however, it has no claws or teeth and is perfectly harmless. It uses a sticky, coiled-up tongue as a furiously fast whiplash to catch insects.

Light and space

San Bushmen, the slight hunter-gatherers who wandered the far-off places of the Namib-Naukluft desert, below, and painted delicate pictures on its rocky outcrops and caves, understood the harmony of nature in which all creatures, great and small, had their place in the immense web of creation. Man, they knew, had no unique rights in this cosmos over the birds of the savanna, the little banded goshawk (*Accipiter badius*), bottom right, or any of the animals of the desert. Yet he could hunt the great kudu like the jackal, right, and all who needed to eat, and warm himself under animal skins as the cool of the evening soothed the furious heat of the day. Man's place was to share in the wonder of life, the clouds and the wind, the laughter of the sun and the peace of the gently falling rain.

A DESERT-DWELLING ELEPHANT, left, will often travel 40 kilometres a day, sometimes by moonlight, in search of sustenance. These elephants can live for up to four days without water which, for an animal that normally drinks 160 litres a day, is no mean feat of determined adaptation. Yet even here there are still poachers, and the dry riverbeds, a vital source of underground water and meagre camelthorn forage for the elephant, are being encroached upon by man and his rather insensitive curiosity.

Like the elephant, most animals have a keen sense of smell. From the dry Kalahari in the east to the cold Atlantic shore there is a whole underground world of small, lightning-quick carnivores that pop in and out of burrow and den to sniff and scent the desert air. The shy, termite-eating aardwolf (*Proteles cristatus*), above, lives up to its fierce namesake only if it is frightened, when it will raise its long dorsal mane and let out a shattering roar.

Also common on the desert sands are hyena, jackal and bat-eared fox. The only true fox of them all is the bushy-tailed and silvery Cape fox (*Vulpes chama*), below. Believed to attack lambs, tens of thousands were systematically hunted and killed in parts of southern Africa. In fact, the dainty fox was unjustly accused: it moves about shyly at night, feeding merely on insects, lizards, shrews, spiders and the occasional wild fruit.

PREVIOUS PAGES: *Heavy storm clouds gather at sunset, a mighty turbulence reflected in the still waters of the Etosha pan.*

*S*alt pan and sky

O STRICHES, RIGHT, ARE THE WORLD'S LARGEST BIRDS, standing over two metres high and weighing up to 90 kilograms. Running flat out across a salt lake or savanna at nearly 70 kilometres an hour, they seem to move like the wind, although they cannot fly. The ostrich's reputation for putting its head in the sand possibly comes from its ability to stop dead in full running stride, drop into a squat and extend its long neck along the ground, effectively vanishing from view.

A male ostrich (*Struthio camelus*) will watch over the clutch of huge, pitted, cream-coloured eggs, each the size of two dozen chicken eggs, guarding them against predators. Young ostriches can run almost from the day they are hatched, and nearly as fast as their parents. Running free and wild is synonymous with the vast open spaces of Africa, whether it be the lopsided gallop of the giraffe, the deceptively sedate canter of the elephant, or the prancing, bucking, stop-and-look-back gallop of the wildebeest, below. And in the finely balanced harmony of the wide land there is also a place for the silent freedom of the yellow pansy butterfly (*Junonia hierta cebrene*), above, the intricately patterned nymph of the veld.

Call of Etosha

Etosha, the "place of the great white spaces", was once a vast shallow lake created, Heiqum Bushman legend tells us, by the tears of a grieving mother. When the Cunene River retreated to its present northern course, the shallow lake evaporated, leaving behind 5 000 square kilometres of salty desert, a mirror expanse of shimmering images, dust devils and the occasional line of lonely zebras trekking endlessly to the horizon.

Grasslands bleached by the sun and acacia woodlands surround the pan, and where there are artesian wells, patient springbok gather to feed on the mopane trees and doze. For the predators, the gathering of animals around a water hole can make for easy pickings. A cunning and competent hunter, the leopard (*Panthera pardus*), top right, is the camouflaged guerrilla fighter of the pan. Nocturnal, silent and deadly, it can penetrate the desert, sticking to the gorges and

tree-lined sand rivers, obtaining the liquid it needs from its prey. It can lift an antelope as heavy as itself into a tree or up a kopje, swim a river and leap three metres onto a rock; it has superb eyesight, and sports extra-long whiskers that help it to negotiate the bush in the dark.

Lion cubs (*Panthera leo*), right, weigh about one and a half kilograms at birth, half the mass of a human child. They are carefully picked up in their mother's jaws when she has to move on, as she often has to do in arid areas where the game are few and as small as this springbok, above. Where lions have to range far to find food the danger to cubs and the possibility of starvation increase, as the adults will eat first from any kill they make. In the dry Kalahari, Namibia and Angola up to 50 per cent of cubs die before they are a year old.

Desert

$\mathscr{S}$*parring partners*

THE ZEBRA'S NAME comes from the Portuguese who first described this "wild ass" in Zaïre 500 years ago. No two zebras' stripes are alike: the colouring is not actually meant to be a camouflage, although it does serve to confuse predators, who find it difficult to single out one animal from the mass of stripes. In the heat of the day a zebra will stand, like a springbok, rump to the sun to reduce exposure. Zebras' habit of remaining close to wildebeest benefits both animals, as the zebras' sense of smell, sight and hearing is an early-warning system against predators, while the carnivores' preference for wildebeest is an inverted safety valve for the zebra.

Although zebra stallions, patrolling the perimeter of family herds and thus exposing themselves to the greatest danger, are very protective when predators are near, they are capable of spectacular infighting when it comes to dominance, ego and the opposite sex. Stallions, right, can clash in spectacular displays of flailing hooves as they rear, wrestle, kick and lunge at each other with bared teeth and slashing hind- and forelegs. They will even drop to the sand on their forelegs and spar ferociously, raking each other's neck with slavering jaws.

As for the cheetah (*Acinonyx jubatus*), bathed in the warm colours of late afternoon above, a San Bushman legend tells of a much more dignified characteristic. There was a race, the story goes, to discover which was the fastest animal on earth, the cheetah or the tsessebe of the grasslands. As they ran, the speedy antelope was just inching ahead when it tripped and fell. The cheetah stopped to help and, as a reward for this kindly gesture, God granted the cheetah the right to be the fleetest creature in the desert.

In glorious pain

BOUNDING ACROSS THE DUSTLANDS in sheer high-jumping celebration of life, the soft cinnamon brown and white colours of the springbok (*Antidorcas marsupialis*) seem to capture the vivacious energy of the plains. The drama of Africa is so often seen in the death of these antelope, or creatures like them: the chase, the fatal lunge, the neck-breaking bite, the inescapable law of kill or be killed. Yet sometimes, in all its beauty, the pageant of the wild is portrayed instead in its beginnings, in birth. The female springbok, right, having given birth to its lamb, will hide it in tall grass for a few days where it remains tightly curled up. Later, mother and lamb will join a nursery herd, the young all resting together while the mothers graze nearby. When summer comes, different herds will join up with one another, forming much larger nomadic groups which were once recorded in herds millions strong in South Africa. Springbok are now generally found only in the dry areas of Namibia and Botswana, although they are extensively farmed in South Africa as game animals.

Wherever you go in the dry mopane woodlands of Africa, perched on top of a small tree you will see a lilacbreasted roller (*Coracias caudata*), above, all brilliantly coloured and seemingly indifferent to your presence. The birds get their name "roller" from their extravagant courtship behaviour. They are common in many other parts of Africa, and one species migrates from as far as Europe.

Communicating down the centuries

WHEN THE LONELY TRAVELLER of the Namibian plains raises his eyes to the great burnt ingot of the Brandberg mountain, left, all hope of succour seems to shrivel in the face of this brooding, lava-tortured rock. But the 30-kilometre-wide and 2 873-metre-high massif, a granite island 500 million years old, is a gentle giant that has, for thousands of years, allowed man and animals to find solace and sustenance among its perennial springs, tough grasses and moringa tree gorges.

Above all, the Brandberg is one of Africa's great treasure houses of spiritual art. The Bushmen were Africa's original ecologists, living in unromantic but total harmony with their finely balanced desert ecosystem. On the rocks and overhangs of the Brandberg there are 50 000 figures of animals and stick-like men and, in the nearby Twyfelfontein mountains, above, another 2 000 paintings and etchings. Other than the tombs of the pharaohs, the rock paintings of the Tassili hills in the Saharan and the fossils of Tanzania's Olduvai Gorge, no one place reveals so much about man in Africa and his relationship with the wild. Bushman painting, painstakingly deciphered in this area by scientist Harald Plager, it is believed by many archaelogists to be largely religious art. It reflects the spiritual potency that man can call on or absorb from certain animals or natural elements during trance dance, an activity that resulted in mutual spiritual healing. It is this healing, this potency, that is portrayed in the designs of the wilderness shelters of the Brandberg, the desert retreat of the Bushman faith.

A twist of sand

THERE IS A PRAYER OF THE NAMA PEOPLE, "Let the thunder cloud stream, O Tsui-goab." It is an earnest prayer, for in the desert this is a rare occurrence. For all the people and the creatures of the desert, drink and food have to be found in other and rather marvellous ways. In the damp cool of early morning, the tenebrionid or darkling beetle (*Onymacris unguicularis*), right, crawls to the windblown, smoking crest of a sand dune, does a hand-stand, and allows the moisture of the overnight sea fog to condense on its shiny back, from where the water then trickles down into its mouth.

Other tiny creatures that have adapted their life to the desert include the reticulated desert lizard (*Meroles reticulatus*), below, which looks like a baby crocodile and feeds on insects on the slip face of dunes. When threatened, it darts away, stops, checks and finally dives for cover beneath the sand. There are also ants which thrive on wind-borne vegetable matter, nocturnal web-footed geckos, and the extraordinary shovel-nosed lizard that performs a sort of thermal dance, lifting first its tail and then each foot in turn off the hot sand to keep them cool.

Possibly the most fascinating of the dune dwellers is the dancing white lady spider (*Heteropodidae leucorchestris*), bottom right. She covers the opening of her dune burrow with a sandsilk web, which is designed to confuse her worst enemy, the black dune wasp. If the spider does encounter the wasp on the dune, it will lurch into a threatening dance that normally sees off the hungry predator. Another dune-dwelling spider, known as the wheeling spider, uses a different tactic. At the approach of a wasp, it heads for the slopes, rolls itself into a ball, and cartwheels down the dune face to safety.

PREVIOUS PAGES: *A quiver tree or kokerboom* (Aloe dichotoma) *stands in the rugged grandeur of the Pondok Mountains. Endemic to Namibia and the dry northern Cape, it is named after the arrow quivers San Bushmen made from the tree's soft wood.*

$\mathcal{T}$he lonely graveyard

THE SKELETON COAST. Even its name conjures up the desolate and ominous nature of this storm-lashed desert coast which reaches from southern Angola deep into Namibia. Gale force winds and mountainous waves terrorize the 550-kilometre-long strip of shoreline, throwing up hidden sandbars that have been the death of many a lonely ship.

Yet the coast, right, also has a wild, spine-tingling beauty. The sea thunders its praise in phalanx after phalanx of spume-thrashed breakers, rolling in without respite from the ocean onto an eternity of rippled surf, sand and fog-shrouded dunes. Some of the dunes, crescent shaped and rearing like a breaking wave, will move up to three metres in a year as their crests, constantly tormented by the southwesterly winds, crash in a roaring avalanche down the slip face.

In the cold seas there are steenbrass, cob and galjoen, while on the garnet sands scuttling ghost crabs play tag with the surf as seagulls and cormorants wheel and dive. Alongside, the bared bones of a broken ship, above, lie testimony to a part of Africa where for once nature is the winner in the terrible conflict between man and his environment.

From a desert came streams

IN THE BITTER VALLEYS of Namibia there are few creatures that do not yearn for running streams. When the waters come, it seems miraculous. Some rivers flow only once or twice in a man's lifetime. Usually they are dry sand beds dusted with the occasional makalani palm or ghostly moringa tree. Yet out of the dry of the endless sand and twisted scrub, the scorched mountain and rolling mirages, the water of life appears.

At first sight, the Fish River Canyon, left, is no green and promised land. Exceeded in size only by the Grand Canyon in the U.S.A., it is a gaping brown scar in the baking pebble plains of southern Namibia, 160 kilometres long and half a kilometre deep. Standing on the edge, the abyss below seems awesome and jagged. Far below where the winds blow, the Fish River sulks, sluggish and green, surrounded by reeds, camelthorns and twisted ebonies.

A people dying, like the waters in a cracked pan slowly evaporating under the merciless glare of the sun, these !Kung Bushmen of the Tsodilo Hills near Botswana's border with Namibia, below, see the ways they once knew disappear. Restricted to a few tourist villages, other cultures have now encroached on these indigenous inhabitants of southern Africa, and there are now no Bushmen left following their traditional nomadic way of life.

Monarch of the dune

BORN TO THE SUN AND THE WIND and the burning seas of sand, the handsome, rapier-horned gemsbok (*Oryx gazella*), right, like its counterpart the oryx dammah of the Sahara, is a true desert dweller. As it runs, its panting causes air to flow past and through a sensitive network of blood vessels in its nasal passages, cooling the flow to its brain, while at the same time its metabolism conserves its moisture requirements, making the animal independent of drinking water for long periods.

The barking gecko (*Ptenopus garrulus*) is a talkative fellow, particularly in the evening when its snappy witch's cackle reverberates over the sand dunes. Somehow it remains elusive, however, like an aural mirage of the desert, its confusing call echoing off the burnt mountains and valleys of pastel gold that mark the Namib sunset. One not so easily fooled is the Péringuey's viper (*Bitis peringueyi*), which lies concealed beneath the surface of the sand, its unique eyes which sit atop its head on the lookout for a meal. As the gecko saunters past, the sand-surfing sidewinder explodes from cover and delivers its fatal bite, above.

War of the worlds

THE HUGE, SINUOUS DUNES at Sossusvlei, left, in their unexpected elevation and ochre colouring, give a richness to the bleak desert. Where the underground Tsauchab River finally abandons its bid to reach the sea, the dunes rise like stars, 340 metres high, the world's highest. Formed by the buffeting of ceaseless winds into perfect whipped-cream formations, they shelter a tiny pan at their base and just enough subterranean water to sustain the old men of the desert sea – spiky, grey camelthorn trees (*Acacia arioloba*). Found growing in forlorn clumps in dry riverbeds, they sprout yellow puffball flowers and pods shaped like camel's ears, furry to the touch.

The giant welwitschia plant (*Welwitschia mirabilis*), below, unique to the arid regions of Namibia and southern Angola, is a marvel of nature, an enduring symbol of the tenacity of life in the harshest of environments. Charles Darwin dubbed it the platypus of the plant kingdom when he first heard of it from wildlife painter Thomas Baines 140 years ago. The welwitschia lives for a thousand and possibly two thousand years, has only two tangled and shredded leaves, weighs up to 100 kilograms and spreads its flouncy corpulence across three metres of sand. It finds much of its moisture through a network of fine roots near the surface, which absorb morning dew or condensation dripping from the plant itself. Young welwitschia are seldom seen, possibly because the pink and yellow flowers of the separate male and female plants can come together only in years of exceptional rainfall. The southwestern corner of Africa seems to specialize in preserving antiquity: the metre-long prints of 200-million-year-old dinosaurs have been found at Mount Etjo, a 60-tonne meteorite, the world's largest, which came to ground at Hoba in the Otavi mountains, and in the same place human fossils have been discovered, to rival East Africa's claim to be the cradle of man.

FOLLOWING PAGES: *The scent of a salty sea enthrals Cape fur seals sniffing the wind at Cape Cross, Namibia.*

 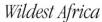

$\mathcal{R}$ainforest

FOREST OF THE FILTERING *dawn, forest of the mists, forest of the high green canopy and the great rains. Forest where life flourishes but, in the gloom of perpetual jungle, remains unknown and mysterious. Here in the vast basin of the Congo River the continent turns from endless open landscapes to huge tracts of equatorial jungle, a feast of thick greenery and colour teeming with plants, animals, insects and birds, from the most delicate flower to great apes. Winding out of its midst, the Congo, or Zaïre, River is one of the few reliable highways both into and out of an impenetrable rainforest, the great band of jungle which stretches in a green swathe for 5 000 kilometres, from the snow-tipped Mountains of the Moon in the east to the marshes of Guinea on the old ivory, gold and slaving coasts of West Africa.*

The heart of Africa

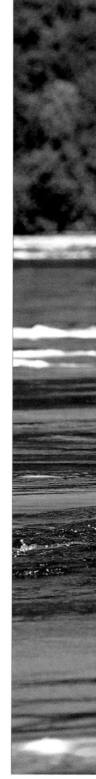

A LL FOUR OF AFRICA'S GREAT RIVERS are associated with the rainforest basin of equatorial central Africa. The Nile flows out of Lake Victoria and through Uganda, the Zambezi rises in the very south of the Mitumba mountain chain, and the massive Congo and Niger rivers flow down into it. The Nile is the longest river in the world, at 6 670 kilometres equivalent to the distance between Amsterdam and New York. In the nineteenth century explorers such as David Livingstone set off in search of the source of the great river, which begins life in south-central Burundi as the Luvironza stream. This flows into giant Lake Victoria and out again as the Victoria Nile, then via Lake Kyoka into Lake Albert, or Lake Mobutu Sese Seko. Between the royal lakes are the Murchison Falls, below, the first of many landmarks on this river's extraordinary journey north to the Mediterranean.

The 120-metre-high falls are formed from three lovely cascades at a point on the Nile where the river is only six metres wide, a cataclysmic explosion of roaring, white-foamed water. It was the River Nile where the Nile or African crocodile (*Crocodylus niloticus*) was first named by the ancient Greeks describing a large "worm" that is fond of basking on river banks, or like this crocodile, right, on a rock at Murchison Falls. Crocodiles feed mainly on fish, although they are known to take large animals and humans, suddenly lunging out of the water, dragging their prey underwater to drown it, then tucking it away under a ledge to keep it safe from hungry neighbours. Like ostriches, they will often swallow a pebble or two to help the digestion.

PREVIOUS PAGES: *Mist drifts over the tall, green rainforest on the Ruwenzori mountains in Uganda, which mesh with the Mitumba and the Virunga chains to form a jagged backbone down the centre of the continent.*

FOR THE FIRST EUROPEANS who went to East Africa, Uganda and the high eastern plateau of central Africa was always the jewel in the continent's crown. It can boast the upper reaches of the Nile, burnt orange above in a smoky sunset, the Murchison Falls, left, and a large chunk of Lake Victoria, as well as a host of lakes and rivers among the high mountains of this green and well-watered land. Virtually a tropical Switzerland, it is a land of rich forests and sparkling water, and is surrounded by magnificent peaks: the Matong of southern Sudan, the Mount Elgon range on the Kenyan border in the east, the **Virunga** volcanoes of the south and, most dramatic of all, the snow-covered Ruw**enzori peaks** in the west.

Huge inhabitants of the Nile, hippopotamuses, unlike crocodiles, are herbivores, usually grazing at night. During the day a hippopotamus (*Hippopotamus amphibius*), top left, prefers to remain in the water, to prevent its thick skin from cracking and burning in the sun. There it will remain, with all but its eyes and ears below the water.

Hippo and crocodile co-exist amicably, for even a hungry crocodile would be foolish to take on the 1 500-kilogram, barrel-bodied, sabre-toothed, roaring, grunting hippo. Despite their aquatic lifestyle, hippos don't swim as such; instead they walk along the riverbed with big, partially-webbed feet.

A fleeting glimpse

IN THE LUXURIANT WET SPONGE of the Zaïre lowlands, a vast, deep drainage basin of a thousand rivers flowing to the Congo, the mist boils up and down as the rain and sun alternately glooms the canopy then throws dappled shade through the labyrinthine foliage. It is here among a wealth of unique and unusual life that the okapi (*Okapi johnstoni*), below, can be found. The word "okapi" means donkey or ass in the language of the small people, the Pygmy hunter-gatherers of the deep forest. Rather like a horse, with its rump and hindlegs striped like those of a zebra, the okapi is a shy, secretive creature with keen senses of hearing and smell developed in its forest environment. It is, in fact, a member of the giraffe family and has that creature's tongue, so long it can give its own eyes a wash.

The Baka Pygmy people of Cameroon, left, are also suffering from a diminishing habitat, forced to live in communal villages and now subject to the degradations of becoming a tourist attraction. Their traditional way of life and social patterns, so intimately attuned to the particular needs of the thick forest are, as a result, dying.

Another member of the rainforest family, the bush pig (*Potamochoerus porcus*), bottom left, is less threatened and fairly widespread. Unlike the warthog, however, which prefers more open country, the bush pig keeps to dense forest cover and forages at night, which tends to make it a rare sight.

Gorillas in the midst of war

THE FOREST OF PERPETUAL TWILIGHT, right, shadowed by almost indefinable trees, leaves and lianas, where the rain beats in repeated drenching on the high canopy, is a botanical treasury of colourful birds, butterflies, a million insects, frogs, lizards and mammals. A tropical rainforest is the true apex of life's wondrous diversity: on the equator, in one acre alone, 100 different tree species will be growing. Under the umbrella of trees, less than five per cent of the sunlight filters down to the understorey where the lianas twist upwards in a hundred spirals and huge ferns relish the thick humidity of the big green gloom.

Born to such a rich habitat, mountain gorillas are shy and prefer to stay well hidden. They are herbivores, never the razor-toothed carnivores of Hollywood's King Kong, and will snack on bamboo, leaves, wild figs, fruits and ferns. Yet by the turn of the century the mountain gorilla could be extinct, a victim of man's continuous wars, poaching, mineral exploration and genuine need for croplands.

A male gorilla, below, weighs up to 250 kilograms, when standing upright is nearly two metres tall, and can live up to fifty years of age. As they grow older they develop white hair on their saddles, giving them a silvery look – hence the name silverback. There are three families of gorillas living in central Africa: the Eastern Lowland gorillas in Zaïre, the Western Lowland gorillas in Cameroon, Gabon and west Zaïre, and the pitifully few mountain gorillas made famous by American researcher Dian Fossey in the high mist jungles along the mountain chain in equatorial Africa that separates Rwanda, Uganda, Burundi and Zaïre.

Women of the forest

THE MOUNTAIN GORILLA (*Gorilla gorilla beringei*), left, was named after Tanganyikan railway construction engineer Oscar Beringe, who caught sight of one in 1902 while hunting in the Virunga mountains. It was to be another 50 years before biologist George Schaller published a major study on their behaviour. Six years later, in 1967, and backed by Kenyan scientist Louis Leakey, eccentric Californian occupational therapist Dian Fossey came to live with the gorillas. She stayed for the next 18 years, a relationship portrayed in the film *Gorillas in the Mist*. The publicity she and Hollywood gave the gorillas has undoubtedly helped their survival as a species, although continuous civil war in the surrounding area is proving a terrible and ongoing threat to these huge primates.

Fossey died violently, murdered in her lonely cabin, but since then another brave woman scientist, Diane Doran, has continued the research. Meanwhile, in Gombe Stream National Park on the shores of Lake Tanganyika in Tanzania, Jane Goodall has spent 30 years doing for chimpanzees, below, what Dian Fossey did for gorillas, researching their lifestyles, adopting, protecting and loving them.

ROODING IN SWIRLS OF CLOUD, the Ruwenzori mountains seem like a dream, a lost world of dripping forests and alpine snows, of strangely outsized plants, glaciers, sudden lakes, mist, boglands and rain. The highest point in the range is Mount Stanley, above, rising above the larger of the two Kitandara lakes. Save for the rocky, snow-patched peaks, thick vege-tation covers the mountain range, as it descends quickly into the thick rainforest inhabited by mountain gorillas, right.

Gorillas in fact live mainly in lowland forests, with only a tiny, if well documented, number living in the mountains of Rwanda, Uganda and Zaïre. They are much-feared animals, and they are still hunted for both their meat and the parts of their bodies sold for muti (medicine). Their hands are made into ashtrays, their skulls used as wall ornaments, and baby gorillas are still shipped to zoos around the world and kept as private pets in many parts of Africa.

It seems cruel that the gorilla, so strong in physique, can be made to seem so weak in the face of man's encroachment, while the delicate, colourful bells of a forest plant such as the clivia flower, below, will flourish in the rich diversity of the yellowwood forest on the slopes of the Ruwenzoris. The strong are made vulnerable, it seems, and the weak strong, in the unending irony and complexity of the jungle.

Origin of the species

W<small>E TALK OF THE DARK CONTINENT</small>. We consider Africa's jungles impenetrable, mysterious and forbidding. Yet we are of them too, for it was from Africa's forests that our primate hominid ancestors emerged to walk upright, fashion tools and hunt on the open plains.

Gorillas and man have a common ancestry dating back 13 million years. The latest evidence comes from Namibia's Otavi mountains which, although now arid, were wet and forested millions of years ago. The recent discovery of a jawbone there indicates that African hominids may not have originated uniquely in the Rift Valley, but instead roamed the whole continent.

The primate family tree is divided into five major groups: lemurs, lorises (bushbabies), monkeys, apes and humans. Humans, the only true bipedal primates, walk upright. Their legs are stronger than their arms which, together with muscular thighs and buttocks, enables this distinctive form of locomotion. The human thumb is also particularly dexterous for the primate family, as it can rotate to touch any finger. The human brain is two to three times larger than that of any other primate and considerably more complex, permitting a high level of reasoning and language skills.

When you see gorillas, such as the youngster below, or chimpanzees (*Pan troglodytes*), right – how they suckle their young, stare wisely at you, a teenager making as if to touch you curiously, occasionally cuffing your leg for approaching too near, and how family groups play and eat together – it is easy to see the familiarity. Down many millions of years Africa, as it does so often, has the humbling knack of reminding us that we are part of nature, not its master.

As intrepid Victorian explorers such as John Speke, H.M. Stanley and Richard Burton searched for the holy grail of the source of the Nile, their explorations allowed a little light to fall on the unknown interior of the dark continent. One of Stanley's discoveries was the lovely forested mountains which the local Bakonjo people called the Ruwenzoris, "where the rains are born". In fact, these snow-capped mountains were known to the ancient Greeks as far back as 450BC, and the pioneering map of Africa designed by Greek geographer-astronomer Claudius Ptolemy around AD150 clearly shows two lakes near the equator, fed by a range of mountains which he called *Lunae Montes*, the Mountains of the Moon.

The foothill forests of these mighty mountains are home to the forest buffalo (*Syncerus caffer nanus*), top left, a smaller and redder version of the plains buffalo, while on the slopes of the Zaïrese Mitumbas to the west, l'Hoest's monkey (*Cercopithecus l'hoesti*), bottom left, with its Elizabethan ruff and mischievous demeanour, is found. It is, however, higher up in the Afro-alpine vegetation zone, right, from 2 500 to 4 500 metres, among precipices, cliffs, bogs and lakes, that unknown riches are revealed. It is a primeval spectacle of forested splendour: tree ferns, slopes of gigantic gold and silver ever-lastings, sentinels of spiky lobelias, rhododendron trees, mosses, lichens, montane yellowwoods, ground orchids, old man's beard trailing from trees, brackens – plants, flowers and trees that in other coastal parts of Africa are tiny "fine forest", but here in the wafting mist and rain and explosive sunlight reach heights many times taller.

Along the languid river

THE HEAVY DOWNPOURS of the equatorial belt constantly feed the exuberant foliage of the rainforest, and eventually the water filters through the undergrowth to a cobweb of smaller rivers, such as the Ubangi, above, which join the Congo River as it winds to the Atlantic in the west. The total catchment area of the river is an area of forest the size of Europe, and on its long journey it carries a volume of water second only to that borne by the Amazon.

The various species of skitterish, agile monkeys, like the white-nosed monkey (*Cercopithecus nictitans*), top right, are familiar creatures of the high canopy which crowds in on the watercourses. Nearer the water itself, countless species of amphibians thrive in the damp environment. Hunted as food in Cameroon in west-central Africa, the goliath frog (*Conraua goliath*), right, is a cannibalistic reptile and, true to its name, grows to sizes larger than a man's hand.

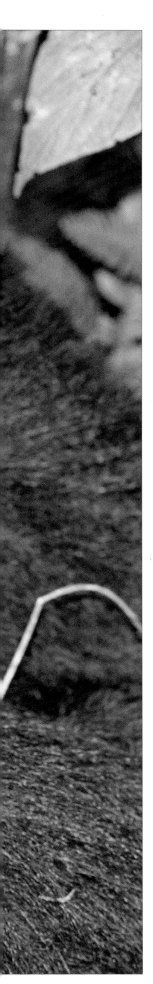

Forest of life

THE RAINFOREST SEEMS TO ENCAPSULATE the vitality of Africa. Everywhere there seems to be growth, a myriad plants, trees, insects and animals. It is impenetrable and unknown, a world apart from the high skies of the grasslands or austere desert, but in energetic harmony the jungle is thriving. The shadowed, damp understorey of the forest contains some of nature's strangest creatures. There are strangler figs that germinate on the canopy and send down aerial roots, flowers that grow on the trunks of trees and are pollinated by bats, gliding lizards, flying frogs, strange orchids and, on the forest floor, the bacteria and minute organisms that are increasingly being used in medical research. Yet mankind and its need for food and space are encroaching on the rainforest at an alarming rate. Of these millions of living things, man manages to destroy one species every hour. By the year 2000 twenty percent of our ten million species on planet earth, plant, insect and animal, could be extinct. We need to provide alternative support for those who have no choice but to survive by slash, burn and plant on the fringes of the forest. If we can do this, if we can genuinely learn to care for our original forest home, then this corner of Africa may prove to be the light of new health and hope not only for the inhabitants of the forest's edge, above, and gorilla, left, but for all the different creatures of the forest, and those who know their true value.

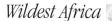

$\mathcal{R}$iver

MILLIONS OF YEARS AGO *tectonic upheavals deep inside the earth shifted and moved a continent. Lava boiled up, mountains were born and rivers were wrenched into new courses. A vast lake was formed in northern Botswana, fed by the Kavango, Chobe, Cuando, Linyante and Zambezi rivers. Then once again the earth rumbled and shifted, shrinking the lakes and forcing the waterways to separate and divide. But the Zambezi, mighty river of Africa, did not forget. For long, heavy stretches upriver, it pretends to sleep, then suddenly, gathering terrifying momentum, it hurls itself wild and free over the black basalt of the Victoria Falls in an exultant mile-wide roar of churning water, spray and mist. The Falls of Queen Victoria, David Livingstone named them.* Mosi oa Tunya. *The smoke that thunders.*

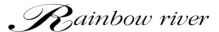

*R*ainbow river

ON 15 NOVEMBER 1855, Kololo polers standing upright in their narrow dugout canoe transported Scottish missionary David Livingstone down the Zambezi to the western side of a flat, palm-tufted island that stands mid-river hovering on the edge of the precipice of water, below. With the falls thundering to left and right of him, diamond spray effervescing in classic rainbows, the explorer spent the night on the island and the following morning walked to the lip of the cataract, then lay full length to peer in awe at the marvellous works of his God. "But no one can imagine the beauty of the view from anything witnessed in England," he wrote, "scenes so lovely must have been gazed upon by angels in their flight." Then, ever the scientist, he tied some bullets from his elephant gun onto a line and lowered it over the edge to measure the height of the falls.

As if in tribute, nature responds to the power of its own reflection, left. The sun-dappled rainforest 60 metres across the chasm from the spot where Livingstone lay is a UNESCO World Heritage Site, an enchanted fairyland of ferns, lianas, vervet monkeys, bushbuck, colourful African birds, butterflies and flowers. It is a joyful chorus of the energy of the water, a forest evergreen and ever-renewed in the drenching upblasts of spray from the falls.

PREVIOUS PAGES: *Haloed by a rainbow, the Zambezi races to the edge of the abyss on the Zambian side of the Victoria Falls.*

Hwange sunset

CONSERVATIONISTS HAVE LONG BEEN AWARE that man's artificially delineated colonial and political boundaries in no way define the migratory patterns or natural home ranges of animals. Yet the survival of animals and even species becomes critical when both the animals and their traditional habitats are subject to different policies regarding protection. If the fences can be removed, a vast consolidated area covering the present reserves of Hwange and Victoria Falls in Zimbabwe, Chobe in Botswana, Namibia's Caprivi and the four huge parks of southern Angola (Mucusso, Luenge, Luiana and Longa-Mavinga), would enable the wildlife of this magnificent savanna wetland to be reunited.

The land does not always appear wet, however, especially in the southern hemisphere winter in June and July, when the low moisture content of the atmosphere is infiltrated by the red dust of the Kalahari sands to reflect a prism of glory at sunset, touching giraffe, left, and pangolin alike with its fire. The metre-long pangolin (*Manis temminckii*), above, which can trace its history back 40 million years, slouches along like some prehistoric war machine. Its array of weapons includes a foul anal smell, the ability to roll itself into an armoured ball which no man or beast can pry open and a tail which it uses like a serrated carving knife cutting back and forth. A shy, nocturnal creature of wooded savanna and wetlands, it is one of the continent's most endangered animals.

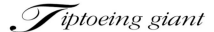

$\mathscr{T}$iptoeing giant

E LEPHANT, OF WHICH ZIMBABWE has Africa's largest remaining concentrations, with up to 22 000 in Hwange and 10 000 in Mana Pools along the Zambezi, are normally seen striding across the veld or lumbering down to water holes, below. An elephant (*Loxodonta africana*) can run at speeds of up to 40 kilometres an hour, hardly making a sound on its cushioned tree-trunk legs, but matriarchs will raise their trunks and scream if they think their young are under threat. On the flood plains of the Mana Pools National Park, the presence of huge applering thorn trees (*Acacia albida*) is responsible for the survival of the elephant along this heavily-forested stretch of the Zambezi. The applering pods and leaves of these towering giants, which form a canopy of silvery lace as you look up at them, are a main source of food for elephant in the dry southern winter season. Unlike most trees, these acacias have a reverse foliage cycle, sprouting leaves in the dry season, letting them fall in the rains. In August and September each tree is laden with nearly 400 kilograms of pods which elephant, standing on their hind legs, left, will reach eight metres into the tree with their trunks to pick.

The tireless river

T HE KAFUE RIVER, WINDING across the plains below, flows into the Zambezi and is typical of the whole riverine system: shallow, sluggish meanderings that run for ever past reed and sand island, forested riverbank, lurking crocodile, snorting hippo, wading birds, and cobwebs of dew at dawn. The "big river", or Zambezi, rises in Zambia and runs along the border which divides that country from Zimbabwe. It is 2 740 kilometres long and produces as much water as all the rivers of South Africa combined.

Vasco da Gama, the great Portuguese explorer, was the first European to see the mouth of the river on the Indian Ocean coast, on 22 January 1498. He named it the "river of good omens" (Rio dos Bons Signaes), yet history has never reflected his sentiment, neither for Portuguese entrepreneurs trying to muscle in on the Swahili gold, ivory and slave trade of the interior, nor for missionary David Livingstone who 400 years later walked the whole length of the river. His wife, Mary, born in faraway Kuruman on the edge of the Kalahari, lies buried in an all-but-forgotten grave not far from the delta where the wind and the salt and the inexorable march of the jungle shore hide her last resting place.

The Zambezi valley, 50 kilometres wide between the smoky blue massif of pyramid-shaped mountains beside the river on the Zambian side and a baobab and mopane tree-covered escarpment in Zimbabwe, is a hot and rugged wilderness. On the alluvial flood plains of Mana Pools the river can be five kilometres wide, and in the dry season attracts vast quantities of impala, buffalo, lion, nearly 400 species of birds, and elephant, right, that amble across the river between the two countries.

Silver sea

LAKE KARIBA ON THE ZAMBEZI RIVER was created by one of the three giant man-made dams in Africa, the Aswan on the Nile and the Cabora Bassa in Mozambique being the others. Each has created new habitats for vegetation and altered the pattern of wildlife. At Lake Kariba the new green swathes of torpedo grass which the "tidal" variations in lake level have encouraged on the lake shores have meant a great increase in the populations of elephant, below, and buffalo (*Syncerus caffer*), right. The changes are evident at Matusadona, which means "place of perpetual dripping dung", with its islands, hazy blue mountains and forests of skeletal drowned trees from which African fish eagle (*Haliaeetus vocifer*), above, swoop to pounce on vundu (catfish).

The highlands of the wetlands

NYANGA, BVUMBA, CHIMANIMANI: a mountain song of windswept massifs 300 kilometres long dividing the high Zimbabwe plateau from the lowlands of Mozambique. Mount Inyangani, right, 2 593 metres high, is the source of a dozen gurgling streams that gather strength and eventually reach the Indian Ocean, some via the Zambezi.

Lake Malawi, above, is the third largest of Africa's great lakes and is linked to the rivers and wetlands of south-central Africa by the Shire River. Its waters flow into the Zambezi, 200 kilometres upstream of the delta, and the lake itself forms part of the Great Rift Valley. In the volcanic upheavals that practically wrenched Africa in two millions of years ago, great chasms such as lakes Malawi and Tanganyika were created, which quickly filled with water. Lake Malawi, which is also called Lake Nyasa, or Niassa, is a tranquil, finger-thin waterway which stretches 600 kilometres up the Rift, almost linking up with Lake Tanganyika. Only 30 kilometres wide, it is a formidable 500 metres deep, with waters rich in fish, its deserted promontories and shores shaded by palms, and beautiful white sands.

PREVIOUS PAGES: *Young boys fishing from the rocks and their canoes at Nkhata Bay on the shores of Lake Malawi.*

$\mathscr{R}$ock of ages

BY THE RIVERS OF *ZHOU*, the word of the Shona people for elephant, the ramparts of Chilojo, left, have for centuries gazed down at the great Gonarezhou wilderness in the southeastern corner of Zimbabwe. The meeting place of the Runde and Save rivers, it has, ever since slaving days, been the free-fire zone of elephant poachers. It has also witnessed the decimation of lofty ironwood trees in an attempt to hold the tsetse fly at bay, the culling of buffalo to protect man's cattle, gun-running, slavery and ivory wars. Every adventurer of the lowveld – Shangaan, Swahili, Portuguese, English and Rhodesian – has had a crack at Gonarezhou.

If you follow the Limpopo River west from Gonarezhou to a point where the Shashi River joins it, then head north, you will soon come to the Matobo hills, above. Visionary imperialist Cecil John Rhodes chose this sublime eyrie as his burial place. Surrounded by massive natural cannonballs, it overlooks a land that seems to have been pulverized by giant blows into a thousand tumbled hills. Great spaces washed by the rain and wind and sun. And silence.

In the summer rains, if Mwari God is bountiful, water courses down these massive granite whalebacks, below, in a hundred glistening streams like the white stripes on a kudu as it pauses among dripping msasa trees. Seventy per cent of Zimbabwe's 13 million people still live and work as small farmers and herdsmen, and for nearly a thousand years they have also mastered the art of shaving off or fire-cracking the surfaces of *dwalas* such as these to produce building blocks. This was how Great Zimbabwe's huge stone structures were made and the same process has allowed modern-day artists in the country to carve exquisite mythological sculptures, recognized as among the most sophisticated in the world.

A river dies in the desert

DUST STORMS SPREAD a canopy of cobalt over these giraffe (*Giraffa camelopardalis*) grazing on Shindi Island, left, one of thousands in the tangled waterways of the Okavango Delta in Botswana. The Okavango is a luxuriant symphony of river, forest, flood plain, lagoon, and ox-bow lake, covering an area of 15 000 square kilometres across northern Botswana and nearly completely surrounded by the Kalahari thirstland. The mokoro dugout, below, is practically the only means of transport along the arteries of the swamp, where the waters are often so clear you can see hippo trails on the channel floor. Ancient watercourses, often dry, link the delta to the Cuando, Linyanti and Chobe rivers that delineate the northern reaches of Botswana, and the remote Makgadikgadi salt pans to the east. All are game reserves with a wealth of animals that include lion, zebra, wildebeest, impala, lechwe, bat-eared fox, buffalo, tsessebe, hyena and kudu. Sitatunga (*Tragelophus spekei*), above, are particularly well adapted to negotiating the myriad channels of the Okavango and its endless palm-fringed islands. The sitatunga, or marsh-buck, swims powerfully in the papyrus swamps, the long, spiral horns of the male almost flat on its shoulders. If pursued by a predator they will stop their delicate tiptoe through the water to bounce away in great bounds and, if wounded, submerge in reedbeds with only their nostrils showing.

RIVER AND DESERT ARE NEVER far from each other in Africa, continent of contrasts and endless vistas, of freezing nights and scorching plains, where all life hangs by a thread and the hope of water. So the creatures of the Okavango flood plains wait, thirsty, patient. In the dry bush they look to their colour camouflage to mask their tracks or hide a stealthy approach. A cheetah (*Acinonyx jubatus*) finds cover, right, even in the green of a wild date palm. If the opportunity for a kill arises it can hurl itself into a 100-kilometre-an-hour chase, but it is easily frightened off by other predators.

Alert over the waters is the malachite kingfisher (*Alcedo cristata*), above left, low-level flyer of the rivers, with its questing red bill and plumage of many colours. It will sit on a drooping reed above a stream or quieter backwater, waiting patiently, then suddenly dive down in a flash of colour at a tadpole or dragonfly. Water shivering off its feathers, it pops back to its perch gobbling the prey head first. To make its nest, the malachite kingfisher uses its beak as a miner's drill, throwing itself head first into a sandy bank and gradually making an indentation, onto which it then clings as it continues the process of excavation.

Every wetland in Africa has as many frogs as fishes, often disguised in psychedelic hues to fool would-be gourmets. There are more than 100 species in southern Africa, of which this painted reed frog (*Hyperolius* sp.), left, settling itself into a water lily, is one. The cheetah and the kingfisher may not change spots or feathers, but the slippery reed frog paints himself in a dozen variations of colour, tone, spots and stripes. What does make him noticeable is a piercing "wheep wheep" call after rains.

River

The twists of life

THE KAVANGO RIVER BEGINS LIFE in Angola, before flowing down through the panhandle of Namibia – an area also known as the Caprivi Strip. Becoming bewildered and disorientated, the river wanders its way into northern Botswana, left, where it almost ties itself in knots as it crosses the sands of the Kalahari, eventually spilling out into the wide fan of the marshy delta.

The marshes, mirrored pools and wide lakes of the delta wetland can make it seem a very still and peaceful place. The abundance of wildlife adds to its beauty, yet in the tranquillity there remains a latent savagery, the sharp point of an African fish eagle's claws as it swoops to take a fish, below, or the teeth of a crocodile (*Crocodylus niloticus*), above, where it skulks menacingly on the surface of the water.

Rumble in the jungle

ALTHOUGH THE FLASH OF brutal savagery can seem sudden and cruel, for the animals of the wild it is no more and no less than their daily fare, the eternal cycles of kill and be killed. A zebra, left, starts with a spurt of dirt in hopeless terror from its most common predator, a lion intent on making a kill. When a predator attacks a herd of zebra, stallions will determinedly defend their own, kicking powerfully in clouds of dust, the zebras barking excitely with a harsh "kwha-kwaha" noise, the lions charging, swivelling, missing, tumbling over. You admire the strength and fluidity of the lioness but your heart is always with the zebra as it defends foal and family.

In fiercer, less one-sided combat, wild dogs, above, attack a spotted hyena in the dying light of the grasslands. Rather than a kill for food, the carnivores are fighting over territory, a vital part of survival patterns for both species. Vicious disputes will also arise between hyena and packs of lion, not always resulting in domination for the large cat, as hyena are far from cowardly and will often tackle lion, using their immensely powerful jaws and razor-like teeth to ruthless effect.

PREVIOUS PAGES: *A thousand blue lagoons, a thousand crystal streams. The great Kavango River searches endlessly for a route to the sea before dying in a panorama of water and aching silence.*

THE WHOLE LENGTH OF THE Zambezi from Lake Cabora Bassa to the Kavango River, some 1 200 kilometres, is a pristine waterworld of game, forests and birdlife. Several large game parks are found along the river system, with others, such as Hwange, nearby. "Hwange" means "peace" in the local Nambya dialect, and it is an area of abundant wildlife and wide vistas, regarded as Zimbabwe's premier game reserve.

All animals take advantage of colour, the time of day and terrain to disguise themselves, as these Burchell's zebra (*Equus burchelli*), left, are doing in the cover of huge trees at sunset. Burchell's zebra like to be near water but will seldom swim in it. When Lake Kariba was flooded many years ago, zebra stuck on little kopje islands would not swim to the mainland and had to be rescued. Burchell, after whom this zebra is named, was an English botanist in South Africa 180 years ago who published two beautifully written and illustrated books on the wildlife and flora he saw during his travels in the interior.

Chacma baboons (*Papio ursinus*), above, move in troops of up to a hundred with large dominant males in charge. Their "waa-hoo" call is the echoey bark warning the troop of danger, especially of the presence of their arch-enemy the leopard. Old males can be bad tempered, and disobedience or disrespect by young will meet with an instant cuffing.

$\mathcal{U}$nder the rising waters

THE ZAMBEZI RIVER, ALTHOUGH checked by the Kariba Dam, continues to run along its ancient course beneath the lake. Enormous tracts of bush were inundated when the waters rose, trapping thousands of animals. Many were rescued by conservationist Rupert Fothergill in his quixotic Operation Noah, which saved 47 porcupine, 12 badger, five wildcat, six scaly anteaters, three hyena and 585 warthog, among 4 914 larger mammals, and many more reptiles, snakes and young birds. The larger animals such as elephant and rhino were coaxed to shore, while lion will swim very well when it suits them.

Along the southern shoreline of Kariba, on the panicum grass plains and green shores, many animals, including buffalo and hippo graze. Buffalo, left, are heavily built animals with great curved horns growing out of a rough black central boss that will dent a tank. They move in herds, grazing and browsing voraciously, sometimes in thousands, but it is the loner with a grudge that is dangerous to

man. In Zimbabwe a professional safari guide cannot get a licence to take visitors walking in the wilds unless he has proved his ability to stop a charging elephant, and later a charging buffalo, with a kill shot in each case. It may seem barbaric but no young man or woman in Zimbabwe may carry a gun to protect his clients without having passed this kill-or-be-killed test.

Of all the feared animals of Africa, hippo (*Hippopotamus amphibius*), above, are responsible for more human fatalities in the wild than any other animal. These huge "water horses", as the Greeks called them, are often seen along the Zambezi. With their massive jaws and tusk-like canines they occasionally chomp a passing canoe in two. Their "yawning" is in fact an aggressive territorial display, but most of the time they will remain submerged, or rise puffing and blowing, eyes above water, pink ears twitching, and calmly watch you float by.

$\mathcal{D}$og days on the plains

Wild dogs (*Lycaon pictus*), above and left, are Africa's most endangered carnivore. Due to man's farms and guns there are fewer than 5 000 left. These beautifully mottled, black and brown creatures are just like domestic dogs, inquisitive, playful and excitable. They hunt in large, exceptionally well coordinated packs, preferring open country where they use their superb sight rather than their sense of smell. To watch wild dogs run down their prey is to watch savage poetry in motion: up to 15 dogs will take turns to tire out a wildebeest, running at 50 kilometres an hour for kilometre after kilometre, snapping at the fleeing beast, tearing chunks off its flesh, until it collapses from sheer exhaustion. The slavering, hungry, yelping dogs will then calmly step back and let their young feed first. A pack is a tight-knit family, all members, not just the mothers, pampering the pups. They communicate by complicated greeting rituals, and there is hardly any inter-pack aggression. Wild dogs will seriously maul any hyena that dares to approach their kill, and leopards also know to stay well away.

$\mathscr{A}$nd all of it is Africa

EVERY FORGOTTEN CREEK, lagoon, backwater and waterway of the vast interlinked river system bounded by the Okavango, the Caprivi, the Zambian plateau, Malawi's great lake and the Zimbabwe escarpment leads, inevitably it seems, to the Zambezi, whose very name conjures up the cry of the fish eagle, the danger, the game, the beauty and the great silences of Africa. It is a primeval riverine world of sunsets and distant mountains and days that light upon the wetlands like the dawn of creation. But it is not all pomp and majesty; it is not only the trumpeting of a bull elephant, the stampede of a thousand buffalo, the lethal lunge of a six-metre crocodile. Nor is it only the roar of rain on the forest, the wind howling across the endless salt pan, the haunting whoop of hyena at night. It is also the place of the little ones at our feet, the small, the weak and the helpless: a myriad flying ants rising after the rains, a dung beetle pushing tirelessly with its back legs, dragonflies hovering in fretful expectation, a spider's web spangled with morning dew. In the waters a wattled crane (*Grus carunculatus*), below, struts with staccato steps, darters (*Anhinga melanogaster*), below right, gather over the darkening, oily-orange waters and a water lily opens its magenta fragrance to the delicacy of a lone jacana (*Actophilornis africanus*), right, tiptoeing on the pancake leaves. Africa.

PREVIOUS PAGES: *Baobab are called the "upside down tree", after a San Bushman legend that God threw one out of his garden and it landed with its roots pointing to the sky. It lives for up to 2 000 years and can have a girth of eight metres.*

A kind of loving

LIFE IN WILDEST AFRICA plays to the continuous, inescapable rhythm of death. In life, the jaunty warthog emerging out of the bush can endear you to Africa, yet in a vicious death it bows to the regal glory of the cheetah, left. No sooner are your emotions kindled than you learn to steel them to the harshness of the wild.

When the land itself bays out pitifully the ache is all the greater, and moments of great sadness and compassion tear at the soul like the teeth of a hungry cat. Above, an elephant, dead on the ground, is not left alone. A companion gently lays its trunk on it, protecting it, refusing to leave, even long after it is dead. It is a kind of loving, a kind of loving in the wild.

Veld

THERE ARE GREAT LANDSCAPES *in the high, hot grassland and semi-desert of southern Africa, empty areas of limitless horizons and huge skies. Across the rolling prairies of wild flowers, dry heat and rocky outcrops, where the African night blazes with icy stars, settlers have come from over the sea from Europe and southwards out of the African interior, in search of space, soil and the once-plentiful game. Beneath the surface of the "veld", or "field" of the Dutch settlers diamonds and gold are mined; on top, cities and roads have appeared – yet there remain here the kingdoms of the veld, the land of the Karoo, the great game sanctuary of the Kruger National Park, and the northern savanna of the Kalahari, parched by drought but home to a wide variety of animals among its dusty grass, tough thorn trees and scattered springs.*

Timeless Kalahari

T
HE LOST WORLD OF THE KALAHARI, or "great drying up" in the local Tswana, stretches 1 500 kilometres across the centre of southern Africa, cut through in its southern regions by the muddy Orange River as it wends its way through the dryness, at one point swirling down an 18-kilometre-long sequences of rapids and gorges known as the Augrabies Falls, above.

Although arid, the semi-desert sustains scattered patches of sweet grass, which provide succulent grazing for large numbers of antelope, as well as cover for animals such as the shy African wildcat (*Felis lybica*), below, peeking out of long grass. It is a close relative of the domestic cat, which are known to have been tamed in North Africa from as early as 3000BC. Springbok (*Antidorcas marsupialis*), right, graze in large numbers on the thirstlands. The dry pan they have gathered around will fill rapidly should the rainbow overhead fulfil its promise of showers, softening the sands.

PREVIOUS PAGES: *The beautiful gemsbok, specially protected in the Kalahari Gemsbok National Park in South Africa, which can survive practically without water, eating tssama melon and scratching the earth for subterranean roots and bulbs.*

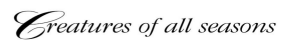

Creatures of all seasons

REMNANT POPULATIONS OF MANY species of animal are being protected in South Africa from both poachers and man's encroachment on their habitats. The last hundred of the great herds of elephant (*Loxodonta africana*) that roamed the Cape in the nineteenth century are firmly safeguarded in the small Addo Elephant Reserve, right, not far from the city of Port Elizabeth. For a while the elephants were fed citrus in the park, but this, as was the case with the provision of meat to attract big cats to tourist viewpoints at lodges near the Kruger National Park, is today seen to be ecologically destructive.

Winter in South Africa can be exceptionally cold at night, with frost, ice, rain and regular snowfalls on the higher slopes. Yet by daylight it is usually sunny and hot, particularly in areas where game are concentrated. The Cape mountain zebra (*Equus zebra zebra*), below, a subspecies of the pony-like Burchell's zebra, was, 60 years ago, about to follow its cousin the quagga into extinction. By 1950 there were only 100 left but they are now protected, particularly in the mountains of the Mountain Zebra National Park in the Eastern Cape, a wild landscape snow-sprinkled in winter and scalded by the sun in summer.

Soaring beyond man and the mountains

CAUGHT AS IF IN A VICE by the huge republic of South Africa around it, the tiny, landlocked kingdom of Lesotho rises up to highlands often called the "roof of Africa". High in the Maluti mountains, left, the bare hillsides are farmed and grazed by the proud Basotho and their tiny herds of cattle or sheep, drenched by the summer rains and cut by the icy cold of winter.

With a wingspan of two and a half metres, the bearded vulture (*Gypaetus barbatus*), standing above beside the smaller Cape vulture (*Gyps coprotheres*), haunts the high crevices of the windy mountains at speeds estimated to exceed 120 kilometres an hour, seldom flapping its huge wings, merely cruising the gusts, the sudden eddies and updrafts of the high, dark mountains. It can feed in flight but prefers to drop bones onto a rock to smash them first, whereupon it feasts on the marrow using its scoop-shaped tongue. As wild game vanished from the mountain areas these birds were obliged to feed on dead domestic stock, so farmers came to see these birds they called "lammergeiers" or "lamb vultures" as scavengers to be poisoned and shot. Today they can be seen in Ethiopia, Tibet, the Pyrenees and parts of the Rift Valley in Kenya and Tanzania; in southern Africa they now number in excess of 600.

PREVIOUS PAGES: *"Karoo" or "garo", the Khoikhoi called it: "desert". The area is famous for its unique rock strata which have revealed fossilized evolutionary patterns of earth's first mammals.*

THE ARID SAVANNA OF THE VELD does not open itself to the rich, bright colours of the rainforest or coast, in a landscape seemingly imprisoned in the repeating shades of sun-sapped browns and dry greens. Yet when the sun falls over the weary land a richness pours from the darkening skies, and the bushland and skeleton trees of the Kruger National Park are held for a few brief moments in proud silhouette. Nesting on the lofty branches of a drowned tree in the still Letaba backwaters, grey heron (*Ardea cincerea*), left, send their harsh, booming call out into the thick evening air.

The bright, dramatically creative patterns used by the Ndebele people bring an intriguing, colourful vibrancy to their small villages and kraals scattered in pockets of the bushveld. It is the Ndebele women, above, who design the intricate beadwork, bright garments and distinctive, angular patterns painted on the mud walls of their homes. Although frequently encountered only in show villages, with the inevitable encroachments of other cultures, the tribe still shows great innovation in their styles and designs, incorporating many modern designs and themes into the traditional patterns.

$\mathcal{T}$*he great white hunted*

CONSERVATION IS CRITICAL in Africa. The rhinoceros, for one, hovers on the brink of extinction, at once threatened by and reliant on man. Not for the first time the hardiest creatures of the wild become helpless in the face of man's careless domination. For many animals, there can be no return to conditions once enjoyed by their forebears, and almost every victory for conservationists is really only a small readjustment in an already heavy imbalance.

Rhino horn has become the cocaine of the conservation business, and although the animals have been de-horned and save-the-rhino campaigns launched, it has been to little avail. There is simply too much criminal money at stake. Zambia, Kenya and Tanzania have largely lost their herds, while in the last ten years Zimbabwe's population of some 3 000 black rhino have been reduced to 300, and this in spite of a ferocious anti-poaching effort that has resulted in the deaths of 200 poachers. Next on the front line is South Africa and the Umfolozi and Hluhluwe reserves, haven to the world's largest concentration of white rhino (*Ceratotherium simum*), right, and where Operation Rhino helped to saved that species.

A plight less known, although no less vital to the continent and her future, is that of the large white and grey wattled crane (*Grus carunculatus*), above, rarely seen now in South Africa. A bird of the wetlands, the wattles referred to are the white dewlaps hanging down on either side of its chin.

THE KRUGER NATIONAL PARK, the pride of South Africa's wildlife sanctuaries, lies in the hot bushwillow, acacia and mopane-tree lowveld 250 kilometres inland from the Indian Ocean, covering a stretch of land to the west of the Limpopo River 350 kilometres long. The Selous Game Reserve in Tanzania, the Central Kalahari in Botswana and the Namib-Naukluft in Namibia are all twice its size but the Kruger is probably the most sophisticated and best organized park in the whole of Africa. It has superb ecological and research departments and a long history of conservation leadership.

It may one day be part of a much larger wilderness, linked to both Mozambique's Parque Nacional de Banhine and Zimbabwe's trans-Limpopo Gonarezhou, a vast area that forms a natural migra-tory triangle for the famous and much-hunted giant elephants of the area. In the meantime Kruger, with its network of good roads, easy access and luxury safari camps, is one of the best places in the world to view the full spectrum of Africa's treasury of game, from this lioness (*Panthera leo*), above, to an elephant, left, drinking from the Letaba River.

Lying as it does in the hot middle ground between the ocean and the high southern African plateau, Kruger does not always get the rainfall it needs to avoid drought. During dry years, even hippo (*Hippopotamus amphibius*), below, which are known to walk many kilometres to find pools, can be left stricken, a sight that dismays even the most hardened professionals in the park.

Of baobabs and baboons

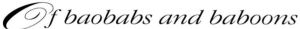

BAOBABS, RIGHT, THE GHOSTLY tree of Africa, are found from the Kenyan coast through to the lowveld riverbed areas of southern Africa. Almost living fossils, some trees are up to 2 000 years old, growing as tall as 26 metres with a girth of more than eight metres, while the bowl of its canopy on top, covered with greenery and huge, sweet-smelling white flowers in the rains, can reach 40 metres.

Baobab (*Adansonia digitata*) pods look like maracas and sound like them when shaken, while the furry seeds inside are quite sweet and tart, the "cream of tartar" used by bakers. The tree's leaves make a tasty relish to accompany samp, a maize-meal staple in Africa; rugs are made from its exceptionally fibrous pith; and it has served as a shelter for more than honey-rich bees. People will actually climb inside a hollowed-out trunk to escape the rain or a predator, and there are records of some trees having served as houses, prisons and storage barns. Dead, dry baobabs have even been known to burst into flame spontaneously. Chacma baboons (*Papio ursinus*), above, will often climb into baobabs to look for water — but not during the lush rains, when the tubers of a water lily are a delicacy.

Eᴸᴇᴘʜᴀɴᴛ ꜱᴇʟᴅᴏᴍ ʟᴏᴏᴋ for trouble – they do not see as well as other animals and if suspicious will lift their trunks to sniff out their surroundings. Upset, they will paw the dusty ground and charge with surprising speed, ears a-flap and trunk hanging down, left. Tusks are used for tearing out chunks of baobab bark if browse is short, and occasionally for fighting over females, although this is usually restricted to head pushing and tusk clashing. Occasionally, enraged, elephants can do serious injury to each other. They can also be intolerant towards other big game such as rhino and hippo. Elephants' huge ears, sometimes two metres long and over a metre wide in adults, expose a maximum area of blood vessels to the air, so that by flapping them they act as built-in air-conditioners for hot lowveld days in the Kruger National Park.

These baby black-backed jackals (*Canis mesomelas*), right, are howling for the return of their parents, on whom they rely for both food and protection. The animal world can often appear ruthless in its treatment of its young and other members of the species, but always it is behaviour born of a greater instinct for survival. Moments of affection are perhaps more rarely seen by man, but they are nonetheless implicit in the nature of most animals. Here a vervet monkey (*Cercopithecus aethiops*), below, patiently grooms ticks off another member of the troop. Ticks are a constant hazard of the long swaying African grass, and tick-bite fever can cause terrible illness in humans, though today is easily treated.

Pʀᴇᴠɪᴏᴜꜱ ᴘᴀɢᴇꜱ: *The Limpopo River enters the Indian Ocean at Xai-Xai in Mozambique. One of its hundreds of tributaries is the Blyde ("joy") River, which in the northern Drakensberg mountains has cut a spectacular canyon nearly a kilometre deep.*

A<small>FTER THE SAVAGE BEAUTY</small> of a skilful kill, the inevitable gore of the aftermath can seem like ugly blood lust. Yet the whole process is simply another aspect of life in the wild, the balance of nature that allows so many different and fascinating creatures to exist together in the bush. In the end, bloodied flesh ripped by a lion's sharp teeth, above, is no more or less a meal than the fresh green grass of the plains is for the wildebeest, in this instance the hunted prey.

In the Kruger National Park a lion's order of preference of food is, by far, giraffe, followed by wildebeest, zebra and impala. An adult male will consume some 30 kilograms of meat at one sitting, skin, bones and all. In other parts of Africa their diet is different, depending on what is available. Lions will take young elephant and buffalo in Botswana, for example, and wildebeest in the Serengeti. At a pinch they will even eat fish trapped in drying pools, and they will feed on mice, reptiles and locusts. Coastal lions, so seldom seen these days, have been seen over the carcass of a beached fur seal or dead dugong.

The leopard (*Panthera pardus*), below, is another fierce killer, a creature of the night that prefers to hunt alone. Meanwhile, metre-tall lappetfaced vultures (*Torgos tracheliotus*), right, will take over after the lions leave, dominating the carcass and chasing all other scavengers away.

$\mathscr{G}$reat tusker

AN ELEPHANT'S TUSKS ARE, perhaps, the feature that gives it such magnificence, yet it is the same tusks that make the great beast so vulnerable to man's greed and selfishness. The largest tusk ever recorded weighed 117 kilograms and was more than three metres long. In India and Burma, elephant regularly use their tusks and trunk to perform hard labour. In Africa, domesticated African elephants such as those at Abu's Camp in the Okavango and Imire in Zimbabwe take visitors on elephant-back safaris.

An elephant, left, has 24 molars which appear in sets of four during the course of its life – as one set wears down, the next emerges. By the age of approximately 65 the last four (weighing four kilograms each) wear out and the elephant usually dies of starvation.

Death at the hands of poachers has been a much more immediate threat to the elephant for hundreds of years, and in some areas authorities have chosen to cut the tusks from the elephants to save them greater harm.

Many animals, like these impala and giraffe, above, will share a drink together at one of the many water holes in the Kruger National Park. The giraffe (*Giraffa camelopardalis*) has a sophisticated capillary system in its neck that prevents too much blood rushing to its head when it performs its rather ungainly stoop to drink. The female giraffe delivers its calf standing up, the infant dropping nearly two metres, the height of a man, to the ground. The foal weighs up to 70 kilograms, or as much as a fully-grown impala.

FOLLOWING PAGES: *The Amphitheatre, a classic sweep of steep Drakensberg mountain-face, seen from the Tugela River as it filters through the rolling foothills of southern KwaZulu-Natal.*

Coast

FLY ON THE WINGS of the dawn, dwell at the seas' farthest end and you will see no fairer sight than the mist-tipped mountains, storm-lashed seas and gentle river lagoons that circle the southern tip of Africa. It is here where whales blow, the fynbos bends to the southeast wind, and the tang of kelp drifts over the rugged shores of the twin oceans that lap this wildest of coasts. To appreciate its many moods, sea and sun, cloud and wind, you have to position yourself in one spot. And pause. It is nothing other than fitting that Africa ends, or begins, in such magnificent grandeur. It is a quintessence of the continent's fragile beauty, one last offering before the waves and ice of the southern ocean cover all. This is South Africa, rainbow coast of hope and harmony, the beloved country.

Coast

The symphony of the vlei

DESOLATE AND BLEAK FOR so much of the year, the vlei, mountain and shore line of the coast are reborn in the Namaqua spring as a million daisies bloom in colourful symphony. Namaqualand is country that receives less than 120 millimetres of rain annually, but when the mid-year showers fall the desert springs to life in an extravagant display of tufted flowers that last until the hot winds of summer arrive to sear the blooms and scorch the land once more. The flowers open in the chilly dawn and close in the evening; on overcast days they do not open at all.

Once one of South Africa's first game reserves (until the game was shot out at the turn of the century), Namaqualand, desert-like and dry, stretches inland from the cold Atlantic on that country's western shore. For a few brief weeks each springtime, it turns into an endless meadow of gorgeous flowers, every touch of the rainbow carpeting the veld in dense clumps, girdling the kopjes and decking the valleys with colour. Seen in a certain light the flowers shine with extraordinary brilliance, like glistening silver on the wings of a dove or snow flashing off a nearby winter mountain.

PREVIOUS PAGES: *From the shores of Bloubergstrand ("blue mountain beach"), looking across Table Bay, Cape Town's Table Mountain rises out of the morning mists enveloping the city below.*

Coastal cries

THE COASTAL WATERS OF THE CAPE teem with crayfish, abalone, seals and penguins. On treasured wetlands and in large shallow lagoons along this chilly, wind-swept western coast, left, a myriad sea birds and waders fill the air with aching cries and the flapping of wings.

The jackass penguin (*Spheniscus demersus*), below, brays like a donkey during courtship on breeding islands such as Malgas, off the Cape west coast. They breed in colonies and swim up to 12 kilometres out to sea to fish for squid, octopus and anchovies, pursuing their prey underwater like submarines, using their wings as flippers. The jackass, South Africa's only endemic penguin, used to breed in millions, but now their numbers are down to an endangered 130 000 as a result of sea pollution and man's exploitation.

Of the 14 species of breeding sea birds in South Africa, one particularly striking variety is the Cape gannet (*Morus capensis*), right. This large sea bird, at 2.5 kilograms weighing nearly as much as a jackass penguin, roosts on the west coast islands in great numbers. They used to feed on pilchards before man deprived them of these, much reducing their numbers, but they still survive on a healthy diet of anchovies. Feeding time is always dramatic, with birds circling above the ocean, then diving and hitting the water like wave upon wave of kamikaze bombers.

The whale's way

THE PLACE WHERE AFRICA tapers off into the ocean is still a home for the creatures of the continent, beyond the long sands and rough cliffs in the vastness of the wild seas. The wide sand-bottomed bays stretching from the Cape Peninsula to Plettenberg Bay along the Cape's Garden Route are romantic bowers for huge southern right whales (*Balaena glacialis*), right and below, which, following earlier calving groups, come into these sheltered waters to mate between the months of August and October. A 17-metre male whale can weigh 67 tonnes, the equivalent of the mass of 12 elephants, the greatest of the land mammals. Southern right whales' courtship is a day-long process which can extend into the night, the female usually remaining on the surface as the male dives and caresses her, trying to coax her sideways to meet him belly to belly. If she doesn't fancy his attentions she will coyly roll on her side or lie on her back, making mating impossible. He will then try to lift her out of the water and re-orientate her, a process that continues until she becomes responsive, whereupon both partners, as if surprised by joy, will begin leaping out of the water, the male doing headstands on the sandy seashore, tail waving in the air.

The southern right whale, with its lopsided, arched jaw, was given its name by whalers because it was the "right" whale to hunt. Its oil content and long baleen mouth sieves, used to strain out microscopic plankton krill, were much in demand and, above all, the whale floated when harpooned.

"TSITSIKAMMA" MEANS "SPARKLING WATERS". The wild, wintry coast of South Africa's Cape that runs along in front of the forested mountains and gorge-crevaced shores of the Tsitsikamma National Park, left, is alternately warmed by the Indian Ocean currents sweeping around from the Mozambique Channel and afflicted by sudden cold fronts moving in from Antarctica and the ice-driven seas of the Southern Ocean 3 000 kilometres away.

Tsitsikamma and the bays near it have some of South Africa's loveliest beaches, with sand-hidden pansy shells in the surf, sea anemone flowers in tidal pools, cathedral rock buttresses, and the ancient mussel middens high above river mouths in the lonely coves that were shelters and sustenance for seashore hunter-gatherers, or *Strandlopers*, thousands of years ago. The fairyland forest itself is a secret world of ferns and tinkling streams, lianas, 40-metre-tall yellowwoods, dark-hearted stinkwoods and, in the deep circles of the forest above the lagoons, Knysna louries (*Tauraco corythaix*), above, flashes of emerald and ruby above the canopy of moss-brocaded trees.

The sounds of the shore

A DRAMATIC FEATURE ON a dramatic coastline, the rock formation known as "the hole in the wall", left, has been hollowed by the relentless, fearsome pounding of the ocean. In the local Xhosa dialect the natural archway is known as *esiKhaleni*, "the place of noise". All along the Wild Coast, this desolate edge of Transkei where the sea boils at the base of sheer, dark cliffs, and treacherous reefs rip ships from the sea, nature seems to be in a vengeful frenzy. Along empty beaches and in the dense woodlands that cover the hills rising quickly above the high cliffs, there is an eerie tone in the sharp gust of wind and growling surf.

Inland and a little farther to the north, in the region which has come to divide the traditional lands of the two most important Nguni people of South Africa, the Xhosa and the Zulu, lies the settlement of Ixopo. To the Zulu inhabitants of the area, such as the girl below with her face painted with a traditional mud paste, the name is spoken *eXobo*, to recreate the sound of someone walking over marshy ground.

$\mathcal{C}$reatures of the wave-washed sand

S EA TURTLES LAYING EGGS ON A BEACH shed great tears, sighing all the while. They have every right to, for the world's eight species of marine turtle are rare and highly endangered, another victim of man's ignorance and inflexibility. As is often the case, the creatures who live most precariously in nature itself are the first to suffer when new pressures arise. Of the eggs this leatherback turtle (*Dermockelys coriacea*), below, will lay, less than one per cent will survive to reach adulthood. A number of creatures stalk the eggs and tiny turtles, including the pink ghost crab (*Ocypode madagascariensis*), right, which skuttles across the silvery sands of the coast.

The leatherback turtle breeds on the Maputaland beaches, near to Kosi Bay, the "river of the dunes of gold". Turtles are slaughtered for their meat, fresh and salted, for the greenish cartilage inside the shell from which turtle soup is made, and for the dappled black and gold carapace of the hawksbill turtle which, polished and shaped, is known as tortoiseshell. Even the yellow, ping-pong-ball-like eggs are eaten. South Africa's determined effort to save the turtle has proved successful, an achievement that is being replicated for the green turtle 640 kilometres off the East African coast on Seychelles' Aldabra atoll.

$\mathscr{T}$he call of the running tide

A<small>T</small> K<small>OSI</small> B<small>AY,</small> <small>VIRTUALLY ON</small> South Africa's east-coast border with Mozambique, an 18-kilometre-long fresh and salt water lake system flanks the beach. Here fishermen have built small kraals with wooden stakes in the shallows to trap fish, left, which are then penned and speared.

For many Africans, it is the coast and the sea, below, that are their wild, endless landscapes. The Agulhas Current flows south from the warmer northern waters of the Mozambique Channel, meeting the colder water and long swells of the south. When a weather system rolls along the coastline of South Africa from west to east against the current, the seas can be thrown into a fearsome turmoil, producing steep, 20-metre waves which have been known to break the back of oil tankers.

Sanctuaries, often dunes of coarse tufted grass, are set aside in places such as the lovely Keurbooms Lagoon in the Cape to protect breeding seagulls. There are 120 species of sea bird along South Africa's coast. Gulls, such as Hartlaub's (*Larus hartlaubii*), above, do not actually dive into the water like true fishing birds but pluck morsels off the surface, especially those from smaller birds that they manage to frighten into dropping their catch.

Coast

A‌H, BUT THIS LAND IS BEAUTIFUL. It was on Christmas morning 1497, nearly five hundred years ago, that intrepid Portuguese navigator Vasco da Gama saw Natal and gave it that name. Sailing past its beaches, its dunes of green forest and strange strelitzia plants, its hills rising in folds with perhaps just a hint of the great shield of mountains in the far distance, he must have wondered at such beauty. Perhaps a sailor aloft pointed out movement in one of the many lagoons: huge elephant shooting water over their shoulders, the clash of ivory echoing through the surf. Later, a wisp of smoke appeared on a hillside barely visible against the dying sun. What people were there? Some clean, fresh water and a little fruit for his salt-hardened crew would be a blessing. But dusk was falling by then, and he would have had to pull out to sea, back into the current that would sweep them onwards to India.

There is a beach, rocky shore and over 200 river estuaries to suit every mood and taste along the continually changing coast. Spread across and around them are plants of infinite variety and delight, like these *Scaevola thunburgi*, right, that both grow in and stabilize the sand dunes. Alongside are tidal pools, above, with their tiny darting fish, black mussels, oysters, sea urchins, crayfish, sponges, seaweeds, sand shrimps and little octopuses that blush brown and pink and scamper away. Yet for all its variety and richness it remains an awesomely fragile beauty, and one that requires special cherishing.

232

The Camelot of the coast

THE CHILLY SUNSHINE FLOWERS of the west coast, the grandeur of the Cape mountains that fall down to the sea, empty beaches shining in the long reach of the waves, the forested garden lagoons and the mighty sea-pounded cliffs of the Wild Coast: each has its own special flavour and scent of the sea.

It is Maputaland, however, above, in the far northeast of South Africa, that is the Camelot of the coast, a land of turtles and lakes, palms and pelicans, ghostly river forests, water lilies, flamingos and gold-spun dunes. Here, where tropical Africa meets the subtropical south, it has the best of both worlds, 21 different ecosystems spread inland and along 200 kilometres of coast. The result is a watery avalon of almost mythical splendour.

Underwater, the reefs of living coral are relatively small but are as extravagantly colourful in the profusion of corals and variety of fish life as the great reefs of the tropics. A loggerhead turtle (*Caretta caretta*), left, glides away into the endless blue, while around the brittle sharp coral there are dozens of species of rockcod or grouper, including the colourful coral trout (*Cephalopholis minatus*), below.

235

LAKE ST LUCIA ON THE KWAZULU-NATAL COAST is really the flooded estuary of many rivers. Home to huge numbers of birds, it is also sanctuary to land mammals which come down to graze on the lush grass, while both crocodile and hippo inhabit the wetlands. Centred five kilometres inland from the east coast, it stretches for 60 kilometres. Golden sands, grasslands, coral reefs and enormous forested dunes, the world's highest, are a few of the showpieces of this precious ecosystem.

As in the animal kingdom, the bird kingdom can boast its own range of the tall, small, mighty, fierce, timid and, of course, clown-like. White pelicans (*Pelecanus onocrotalis*), right, or *iVubu* in the local Zulu, cruise like low-flying assegais in solid "V" formation when they herd and trap fish into a shallow corner on the waters of the St Lucia lakes. They take up great scoops of water catching their fish, squeezing out the excess water before greedily gulping down the morsels. The white pelican, which is known in Asia and southern Europe, can weigh up to 15 kilograms; the pink-backed variety which is confined to Africa is much smaller.

From the jester to the prince. Around the southern coastline of Africa one of nature's most delightful and attractive creatures, the dolphin, is often seen playing around boats or by the curling lip of the breaking surf. Bottlenosed dolphin (*Tursiops aduncus*), above, are found in both Indian and Atlantic oceans, the great seas which meld under the proud gaze of rugged Cape Point on the very southwest tip of the continent.

FOLLOWING PAGES: *Cape of storms, fairest Cape, wildest Cape. But, above all, Cape of Good Hope.*

240